CALVINISM CHALLENGED

By Dr. Al Garza

Published by Sefer Press Publishing

How The Hebrew Bible, Jewish Sources, Jesus, The Apostles and Paul Refute Calvinism.

Copyright©2018 All Rights Reserved

Publication rights Sefer Press Publishing House
Questions & Comments; SeferPress@israelmail.com

Publisher grants permission to reference short quotations (less than 400 words) in reviews, magazines, newspapers, Web sites, or other publications in accordance with the citation standards at Sefer Press. Request permission to reproduce more than 400 words to SeferPress@israelmail.com

Cover by Sefer Press 2018

Book Format by Sefer Press 2018

ISBN: 978-0-692-19729-5

For questions or comments, please write to

SeferPress@israelmail.com

Bible Abbreviations

Bible translations is that of the author who translated from the Hebrew and Greek languages if Bible sources not shown.

Printed in the United States of America 2018

TABLE OF CONTENTS

Introduction..................4

Creation and the Fall.............9

The Serpent..................12

Sin......................22

Noah and the Flood............26

Noah and Grace...............34

The Sovereignty of God and Man.51

Choose Life..................59

God is in Control..............64

2nd Temple Period and the NT......70

The New Testament.............75

John 6:37-45.................78

John 12:27-33................83

Eph.1:1-11 and Rom.Ch.7-11......87

Rom. 9: Salvation or Judgment?..95

Conclusion...................103
Appendix A: John 1:13..............105
Appendix B: Acts 13:48............109

INTRODUCTION

The idea of how God saves his people from their sin has been in debate for centuries. In modern times there have been only two camps of thought, the Calvinist view, and the Arminian view. These two views seem to rise from the ashes around the 15th century before gaining popularity in the [1]16th century. Some have even proposed the teaching of Calvinism goes back to Augustine. But before Augustine, there is no support for reform Calvinistic teaching. [2]Loraine Boettner, who is a Reformer, explains in his book, *"It may occasion some surprise to discover that the doctrine of Predestination was not made a matter of special study until near the end of the fourth century."* He goes on to say the early church fathers focused on good works, faith, repentance, almsgiving, prayers, and submission to baptism as the basis of salvation. Boettner concludes by saying, *"They of course taught that salvation was through*

---

[1] In the context of the Reformation, Huldrych Zwingli began the Reformed tradition in 1519 in the city of Zürich.

[2] *The Reform Doctrine of Predestination,* Loraine Boettner; pg.365

Christ; yet they assumed that man had the full power to accept or reject the gospel." Did the early believers *assume* man had the power to accept or reject the gospel? Or is Boettner drawing his conclusion based on his reform position? The majority of Calvinist believers will refer to the Bible for support of their position within reform theology. But if Boettner is correct that such a teaching was not made a special study before the fourth century, then predestination, as taught within Calvinism, cannot be supported by the Bible and must be understood as a man-made doctrine and teaching.

    The two leading modern teachers of Calvinism is John Piper and James White. Both of which I will be referring to in this book. There are many different thoughts on Calvinism and what it teaches regarding salvation. Some Calvinist believe that God elects some for heaven and some for judgment. Others will say that God elects some to believe by his grace but passes over others who will be judged in the end. I will be using the works of Piper and White for definitions and terms regarding how God saves individuals. I will be first looking at the fall of man and the Hebrew understanding of sin and man's responsibility. Before looking at the New Testament, we need to have a firm foundation of the Hebrew Old Testament. The New Testament must be interpreted by the Hebrew Scriptures since it is the foundation for the New Testament. [3]Paul the apostle when talking about the Hebrew Scriptures said, "*All Scripture is breathed out by God and profitable for teaching, for reproof, for correction, and for training in righteousness...*" The Scripture breathed out by God is the Hebrew Old Testament. We must use it to teach, reprove and correct men who have a different doctrine. I must stress that our differences in belief in regards to how God saves should not be used to divide believers in Yeshua-Jesus or to condemn those who disagree on either side. I say this in regards to the Hebrew Scriptures because the majority of Calvinist when defending the doctrine of salvation use the New Testament as their foundation before even looking at the Hebrew Old Testament. They look at sin and grace from the Greek, not realizing that both are rooted in the Hebrew Scriptures. A false view of sin and grace in

---

[3] 2Timothy 3:16 ESV Translation.

regards to man and salvation is where the errors begin. A Greek Western view of the Bible as a whole is a wrong way to approach the doctrine of salvation when the Bible itself was written by [4]Jews who were entrusted to preserve it in the language of Hebrew. When we forget this fundamental fact, we are left to interpret the Bible our way.

In this book, we will be trying to answer two important issues about salvation. Does God elect some for salvation with grace and elect or pass over others for judgment? Is God sovereign over his creation including their decessions for coming to him for salvation? Or does man have a choice to come to God by their own will while God still being in control of his creation? Since God entrusted the Jews with his teachings, what teachings were given to them to entrust? Were those teachings the same we find in Calvinism or are those teachings consistent with the Jews who preserved God's word? Namely, that man has a choice to come to God and his son Yeshua-Jesus

---

[4] Rom 3:2. "Yes, the Jews have many benefits. The most important one is this: God trusted the Jews with his teachings." ESV

for eternal life or to face his curse in death and judgment.

    To begin this discussion, we must start from the beginning and look at creation and the fall of man. We must define sin from the Hebrew language and how God defined it to Moses. We must define grace the same way too. This approach will give us a foundation of both terms and how they were used during the time of Moses. We also need to understand that both words had changed in meaning when they were translated into Greek after the Jews returned from exile from Babylon. The Greek language is abstract while Hebrew is a concrete Semitic language. An example of this is the fact that the very name of God is lost when translated into Greek. You cannot translate the name "YHVH" into Greek without losing its origin and meaning in Hebrew. This is also true of the Hebrew word for sin and grace. Let us start from the beginning with God's creation and the fall of man.

CREATION AND THE FALL

To get a good understanding of the fall of man and sin, we must look at the beginning of creation itself. Moses wrote the first five books of the Bible called the Torah in Hebrew. They are Genesis, Exodus, Leviticus, Numbers, and Deuteronomy. We must first understand that Moses is writing exactly what God told him to write from Genesis to Deuteronomy. The stories in Genesis are spoken to Moses by God himself. We do not know how much Moses already knew from oral tradition that might have been handed down by the Hebrew people while in Egypt or even before being enslaved. So even though Moses is writing down the events, it is God himself who is the source of the stories from the beginning.

[5]*"In the beginning, God created the heavens and the earth."* (Gen.1:1)

---

[5] Gen 1:1 בראשית ברא אלהים את השמים ואת הארץ

These are the opening words to the book of Genesis. Let me first point out that this is not the best translation for the word *created*. The word *created* should be translated as *formed* or *shaped* the heavens and the earth. Some scholars believe that God created the heavens and the earth out of nothing. God simply spoke everything into existence. It should be understood that God also *created* man from the dust of the ground. The same Hebrew word is used in both Genesis 1:1 and Genesis 1:27, *bara*. So, did God create man out of nothing or did he shape and form man from the dust of the ground as described in Genesis 2:7? The answer is simple; God-shaped and formed man the same way he shaped and formed the heavens and the earth. But why? The very next verse of Genesis answers that very question.

[6]*"Now the earth was formless and empty."* (Gen.1:2)

The earth was formless and empty, so God-shaped and formed the earth and filled it with living creatures and

---

[6] Gen 1:2 והארץ היתה תהו ובהו

humanity. This is how Genesis reads in the first 27 verses. Everything that exists in the heavens and the earth was formed by God, including the spirit hosts of heaven. This is what you read in Psalms 33:6, *"By the Word of the YHVH the heavens, were made, and by the breath of his mouth all their host."* This is the same *Word* that became flesh in John 1:1 and who Paul, the Pharisee trained under Gamaliel, declared concerning the Messiah Yeshua-Jesus in Colossians 1:16, *"For by him all things were created, in heaven and on earth, visible and invisible, whether thrones or dominions or rulers or authorities – all things were created through him and for him."* The very Word of YHVH and who is also the Messiah Yeshua-Jesus also created the heavens and the earth and everything in them. So now that we have established that everything that exists in heaven and on earth was created, formed and shaped by God which would include the spirit hosts of heaven, the question remains, did God create spirit forces who would follow him or did they chose to rebel against him? To answer this question and others, we need to look at the fall of man and the cause of such a great event.

The Serpent

After the man was formed from the ground, the Bible says that God planted a garden in a place called Eden in the east. In other places in the Bible, the Garden of Eden is described as the Mountain of God and the Garden of God. Before the fall everything was good after God finished his creation. In this garden and mountain of God, there were two trees placed in its midst. There was the tree of life and the tree of knowledge of good and evil. As we will learn later, the tree of life was created to keep both the man and the woman alive forever. As long as they ate from that tree, they would never die. So what was the tree of knowledge of good and evil all about? Why did God create a tree that would cause both of them to disobey him and disrupt all of the creation? The answer is simple, the freedom to choose. Without the tree of knowledge, man and woman would only be able to be in a relationship with God because God made them do so. With the tree of knowledge, they both now have the ability to choose for themselves life or death. This is what we continue to find after the fall when God tells his people in Deuteronomy 30:19, "*I call heaven and earth to witness against you today, that I have set before you life and death, the blessing and the curse. So choose life in order that you may live, you and your descendants,..."*. God set before them life and death as he did back in the garden. The blessing and curses are still in effect after the fall with humanity having to choose either one. As we will see later, the blessing of life comes only through Yeshua-Jesus when we choose life in him for eternity.

Another word we must understand is the word *knowledge*. The Hebrew word is [7]*da'ath* and means not just to know something but to *discern* and *understand* with wisdom. The tree would give the man and woman the ability to discern and understand what is good and what is evil. Both good and evil have special meaning in Hebrew too. In the simplest form, [8]*good* means something that is beneficial for well-being while [9]*evil* means distress, misery, and calamity. They would have the ability to create and form good or evil for

---

[7] BDB Definition: 1) knowledge 1a) knowledge, perception, skill 1b) discernment, understanding, wisdom.

[8] NASEC a good thing, benefit, welfare טוֹב

[9] NASEC evil, distress, misery, injury, calamity רַע

themselves. Something only God could do at the time. After the fall God still reminds us through the prophet Isaiah when he writes, *"I form light and create darkness, I make well-being and create calamity, I am the LORD, who does all these things."* This brings us to the serpent who was in the Garden of Eden and dwelling on the tree of knowledge.

There have been many attempts to try and explain what the serpent was and how he ended up on the tree of knowledge to cause the fall of man. I will make the same attempt but only relying on what the Bible says and from the Hebrew understanding. The first time the serpent appears in the Bible is in Genesis 3:1 where we read, *"And the serpent was cunning above every beast of the field which YHVH God had made. And he said to the woman, 'Is it so that God has said, You shall not eat from any tree of the garden?'"* The first thing we notice is that the serpent is compared to every other beast in the field that God made. This leads us to believe that it was a reptile of some kind that was made by God directly. Some scholars believe that the serpent was not a beast or snake-like creature but some kind of supernatural being like Satan. There is nothing in the context of Genesis 3 to suggest such a view. In fact, every time the word *serpent* is used in the Bible, it is used to identify a reptile who bites and hisses. This is based on the Hebrew word for *serpent* which is *nachash*. The serpent is no different than the other beasts except in one area. It was more crafty than any beast of the field. That Hebrew word for [10]*crafty* can also be translated *sensible* and *prudent*. The Bible does not explain how this serpent was able to talk to the woman. It seems that before the fall this was possible. The serpent later in history will become the object of worship in many [11]cultures including Taautus, or the Egyptian Thoth, who was the first that attributed deity to the nature of the dragon, and of serpents; and after him the Egyptians and Phoenicians: the Egyptian god Cneph was a serpent with a hawk's head; and a serpent with the Phoenicians was a good demon.

    The woman was deceived by the serpent as Paul

---

[10] BDB Definition: 1) subtle, shrewd, crafty, sly, sensible ערום

[11] "Storytelling, the Meaning of Life, and The Epic of Gilgamesh". eawc.evansville.edu. Archived from the original on 2011-11-30. Retrieved 2017-11-27.

tells us in 2Cor.11:3, *"But I am afraid that, as the serpent deceived Eve by his craftiness, your minds will be led astray from the simplicity and purity of devotion to Christ."* Some would suggest that the serpent lied to the woman, but the Hebrew does not say the serpent lied but that she was deceived as Paul states and the woman herself told God that she was deceived, Gen.3:13. In short, the woman believed that if she touched or ate the fruit, she would die immediately as if she was poisoned. But earlier God told the man that if he ate from the tree, he would eventually die as a punishment for disobeying. The Hebrew [12]grammar makes this clear. The woman was wrong in thinking it was like eating something poisonous while the serpent corrected her by telling her that God did not say that. The serpent did not tell her what God said which lead the woman to believe that it was okay to eat from the tree. The serpent did tell the woman that if she ate from the tree, she would be like God, knowing good and evil. It appears the role of the serpent was to try and persuade either the man or the woman to eat of the tree that God had told them not to

---

[12] Gen.2:17 מות תמות vs. Gen.3:3-4 תמתון מות

eat. Again, since God created everything good we have to assume the serpent was created good but with the role of being a deceiver for the sake of choosing life or death. Without the serpent and the tree of knowledge man and woman would be preprogrammed for only one thing, to serve and love God without a choice. In essence, love is not loving at all to be created without a choice but points to being slaves to God.

After the man and the woman ate from the tree both of them knew they were naked because now they could discern what was good for them and what was harmful toward them. They became afraid and ashamed of how God created them and covered themselves with fig leaves. When God speaks to them, the man tells God that it was the woman who gave him the fruit from the tree and the woman tells God that it was the serpent who deceived her into eating the fruit. At that moment God tells the serpent the following, *"YHVH God said to the serpent, 'Because you have done this, Cursed are you more than all cattle, And more than every beast of the field; On your belly you will go, And dust you will eat All the days of your life;'"*, Genesis 3:14. [13]In Jewish tradition, it was believed that the serpent might have had legs or was more upright until God cursed it on its belly. So why did God curse the serpent if he created him to be crafty? I believe the serpent was punished for not telling the woman exactly what God told the man and let her assume the tree was good to eat. The serpent knew the truth and even told the woman that she would become like divine beings if she ate of it. All that was true, but the serpent did not tell the woman that if she ate she would eventually die physically in time. The serpent withheld information from the woman.

    I remember a time when I was at church and was thinking about going to a Bible study that was being held that night by one of the members of the church. I asked one of the other members that I had heard that it was going to be canceled and nobody was going, according to the one who was having the study at their house. The member looked at me and said, *"No,*

---

[13] John Gill's Commentary on Gen.3:14; Midrash Rabbah Genesis vol.1 pg.162

Jeff did not say that, in fact, we are supposed to finish the book of Acts too." Now, the member withheld the fact that Jeff said that he might not be home tonight due to some work issues. The member wanted me to show up, so he decided not to tell me what Jeff said and allowed me to decide to show up at the house. Did the member lie to me? No, he just withheld what Jeff said and let me choose to go or not. In all fairness, I did not go and confirm for myself what Jeff said.

The serpent asked the woman a question that was partially true in its form. *"Did God say, 'You shall not eat of any tree in the garden'?"* No, God said they can eat from any tree in the garden except for one tree that was in the midst of the garden. The woman knew the answer but did not know why she could not eat of that one tree. The *any* was *one* tree that was in the Garden of Eden. The serpent was cursed for withholding what God said regarding the tree and its true consequences for eating it.

After the curse of the serpent, both the man and the woman were removed from the garden and placed outside of it. The man had to work the ground for food in pain for the rest of his life until he returned to the ground in physical death. The same ground where God created man. The tree of life was no longer available to eat. [14]God knew that if they ate from the tree of life, they would live forever with his knowledge of good and evil. Physical death was always present in their bodies, but it was dormant because of the tree of life. Those within the reform movement and Calvinism would have us believe that the man and woman suffered spiritual death and not just physical. There is nothing within the Hebrew language of Genesis chapters 2 and 3 that suggest spiritual death. The entire context is on physical death as the penalty for disobeying God. The "spiritual death" teaching has no support from the Hebrew language but is an invention within reform theology to explain the need for a spiritual regeneration from God. In fact, the Hebrew word for [15]"death" only has one application in the Bible, and that is toward physical death. It never refers

---

[14] Gen 3:22 "Then the LORD God said, 'Behold, the man has become like one of Us, knowing good and evil; and now, he might stretch out his hand, and take also from the tree of life, and eat, and live forever.'"

[15] מות BDB Definition: 1) to die, kill, have one executed [always physical]

to a spiritual death of any kind. The word "spiritual" never has a connection with "death" in the Hebrew Old Testament. The term "spiritual death" is part of Calvinism called Total Depravity. Total Depravity is grounded on the false term *spiritual death*. Without spiritual death, Total Depravity fails. Even Calvin himself in his commentary on Genesis 3 believed in the physical death of men and not the spiritual death when he says, [16]*"But it is asked, what kind of death God means in this place?... Death, therefore, is now a terror to us; first, because there is a kind of annihilation, as it respects the body;... For then was Adam consigned to death, and death began its reign in him, until supervening grace should bring a remedy."*

[17]James White makes this point, *"The 'flip side' of divine freedom is the fact that man, the great image-bearer of God, is a fallen creature, a slave to sin, spiritually dead, incapable of doing what is pleasing to God."* We need to look at the word sin in relation to man and determine if James White is correct.

---

[16] Commentaries on The First Book of Moses Called Genesis by John Calvin Volume 1

[17] *The Potter's Freedom*, Jame R. White. Calvery Press Publishing pg.76

SIN

Calvinist suggests that when people sin it is because they are spiritually dead and a slave to sin. That still begs the question, what is *sin* and who is responsible for it, if any? To understand what *sin* is we must first look to the Bible and see when the word was first used. The first time *sin* appears in the Bible is Genesis 4:7, *"If you do well, will you not be accepted? And if you do not do well, sin is crouching at the door. Its desire is for you, but you must rule over it."* The ancient Hebrew two-letter root word for *sin* is "CHeT" with a *CH* sound like the word Ba*ch* and *Tet* at the end. [18]The Hebrew picture of *sin* is a fence and a serpent. The ancient Hebrew word picture takes us right back to the garden with the serpent who deceived the woman to cross over and disobey God. Picture the serpent on a fence trying to deceive you as if the grass is greener on the other side of the fence. If you go then, you have sinned against God who told you not to go. The basic

---

[18] *Hebrew Word Pictures*, Dr. Frank Seekins, pg.40;44;208 quoting Gesenius.

understanding of the word *sin* is to disobey God and miss the mark. But as God said, you must [19]rule over sin. Even Paul in the NT had this same understanding regarding sin when he said in Romans 6:14, *"For sin shall not be master over you, for you are not under Torah but under grace."* To sin is a direct action against God which comes back to the one who sinned. In regards to Genesis 4:7 all the [20]Aramaic translations say, *"...your sin is reserved to the day of judgment,"* or as [21]Rashi, a Jewish Rabbi puts it, *"...lies at the door of the grave, reserved to that day."* Because of sin, we are heading to the grave in physical death. Sin and death go hand and hand. You can not understand or speak about one without the other. As Paul said in 1Cor.15:56, *"The sting of death is sin, and the power of sin is the Torah;"*

    We must understand, Moses does not tell us why the man ate the fruit, but we do know the woman was deceived. The word *sin* does not appear until God speaks to Cain in Genesis 4. We will read later how

---

[19] NASEC-a prim. root; *to rule, have dominion, reign, gain control.* מָשַׁל

[20] *Onkelos on the Torah:Understanding the Bible Text*, Genesis pg. 22

[21] *Onkelos on the Torah:Understanding the Bible Text*, Genesis pg. 22

Jews began to answer some of the questions of *sin* during the 2nd Temple era. *"Therefore, just as sin came into the world through one man, and death through sin…,"* Romans 5:12. The fall of man does not answer the origin of sin completely. The man and woman were created to be a child-like person without the complete knowledge of good and evil. That discerning between both is god-like wisdom and knowledge that belonged to God and God alone. Anyone can look at the news daily, and see the result of having such knowledge and the damage that it can do to the world. We have obtained what should have belonged to God.

      What have we learned so far? We have read that God created two trees in the garden. One tree was the knowledge of good and evil while the other was the tree of life. God gave the man his first command to not eat from the tree of knowledge. So the man had a choice right from the beginning. After he disobeyed God, he was cast out of the garden and forbidden from eating the tree of life. This already proves the man and the woman would have a choice even after both were removed from the garden with the knowledge of good and evil which belonged to God. They would continue to live out the rest of their lives with the knowledge of good and evil and would then be able to choose how to act with that knowledge. But what is the true intent of man and is man responsible for his actions?

NOAH AND THE FLOOD

As we begin to look at Noah and the flood, we must understand the different views of what caused God's judgment to bring the flood upon mankind. The first four verses of Genesis 6 has been debated by both Jews and Christians for the last 2000 years. Let's look at them below.

"And it came to pass when men began to multiply on the face of the earth, and daughters were born unto them, that the sons of God saw the daughters of men that they were fair; and they took them wives, whomsoever they chose. And the LORD said: 'My spirit shall not abide in man forever, for that he also is flesh; therefore shall his days be a hundred and twenty years.' The Nephilim were on the earth in those days, and also after that when the sons of God came in unto the daughters of men, and they bore children to them; the same were the mighty men that were of old, the men of renown.", Genesis 6:1-4.

So what does this have to do with Calvinism and Reform theology? First, many modern Christian scholars have used these verses to try and demonstrate that fallen angels, sons of God, came down to earth and took wives for themselves and had children with them. This unholy act caused a hybrid mix of half human and half divine being which somehow survived the flood and managed to keep reproducing to this day. The understanding is that the fallen angels are part of Satan's army and a band of demons. The Christian and some Jewish scholars see "sons of God" as a title for divine angelic beings. Now let me say that not all Christians hold this view nor do all Jewish scholars. In fact, during the 2nd Temple era, the Dead Sea Scrolls, and in later Jewish literature, we will see later on, the view of *sons of God* being angels was in debate. Let us first look at the plain meaning of the text from the Hebrew and see if angels are a good interpretation of that explanation.

The events leading up to the flood are mentioned in Genesis 4 and 5. When Cain was sent into exile away from God, he settled in Nod, east of Eden, Genesis 4:16. From that point, we have the genealogy of Cain's descendants ending with Lamech. Cain's line does not seem to be righteous but wicked. Remember, Cain was no longer in the presence of God. In that line, we read about Lamech who says he killed a man for wounding him and a boy for striking him. From there we are told that Adam had another son named Seth. It is at this point where after Seth has a son that the passage says, *"To Seth also a son was born, and he called his name Enosh. At that time people began to call upon the name of the LORD."* Genesis 4:26, ESV. The Hebrew does allow for another type of reading. *"Then began men to call themselves,"* or *"to be called by the name of YHVH."* This understanding of Seth and his son Enosh being called sons of God or by his name, YHVH, is not foreign to the Bible. In Deuteronomy 14:1 Moses tells the people, *"You are the sons of YHVH your God."* Even in the New Testament in the gospel of Luke, we read the genealogy of Joseph all the way back to Adam who is called the *Son of God*, Luke 3:38. There seems to be a clear distinction between the genealogy lines of Cain and Seth. The genealogy of Seth ends with Noah and his three sons, Genesis 5:32. So if the line of Seth were called sons of God and then when we read Genesis 6:1-4, we can easily see the sons of God being men from the line Seth and not angels. In fact, the whole context of

Genesis 6 is about the wickedness of man. *"YHVH saw that the wickedness of man was great in the earth and that every intention of the thoughts of his heart was only evil continually."*, Genesis 6:5. God destroys the earth by the flood because of the wickedness of man. There is no hint or suggestion to suppose that the sons of God are anything more than men in the context. This is why you have a distinction in the verse of *sons of God* and *daughters of men* or sons of men. Cain and his descendants were exiled from God while Seth and his descendants were still with God and Adam.

According to other [22]sources, immediately after the death of Adam, the family of Seth was separated from the family of Cain. Seth took his sons and their wives to a high mountain (Hermon), on the top of which Adam was buried, and Cain and all his sons lived in the valley beneath, where Abel was slain, and they on the mountain obtained a name for holiness and purity and were so near to divine beings that they could hear their voices and join their hymns with them

---

[22] *John Gill Commentary Gen.6:2*, Elmacinus, Patricides apud Hottinger. Smegma, l. 1. c. viii. p. 226, 227, 228.

and them, their wives and their children, went by the common name of the sons of God. Now, these were adjured, by Seth and by succeeding patriarchs by no means to go down from the mountain and join the Cainites but notwithstanding in the times of Jared some did go down and take wives to have children. It is only in later Jewish tradition that we find views of angels and fallen watchers put back into the text. These are later interpretations that are picked up by the western churches and in Christianity.

This takes us to the word "Nephilim" in Genesis 6:4. This word is predicated on the notion that *sons of God* are, once again, fallen angels or divine beings from heaven who came down and took wives for themselves. Genesis 6:4 reads, *"The Nephilim were on the earth in those days, and also after that, when the sons of God came in unto the daughters of men, and they bore children to them; the same were the mighty men that were of old, the men of renown."* The Hebrew word *Nephilim* comes from the Hebrew word *naphall* which means *to fall*. Another Hebrew word associated with Nephilim is *nephil* which refers to a tyrant or a giant. These fallen tyrants who were giants were just men, mighty men, and men of renown or authority. The Hebrew allows for such understanding. From this point on Moses tell us of the wickedness of man that God saw and man's intent in doing evil from his heart was continually going on in the earth.

I need to mention that the Hebrew word for [23]*intent* is *yatser*, in Genesis 6:5, and refers to man's own forming or framing of doing evil. It is man and man alone who intends to do evil and is forming the thoughts in his mind and heart. This is what we read earlier at the fall of man. God did not create man to do evil and some to do good as some Reformers suppose. The result of man's evil intent comes from the tree of knowledge of good and evil with man's freedom of choice as we have seen. In later 2nd Temple [24]Jewish literature Jews who wrestled with this idea began to develop and create other answers such as demon influences that caused a man to do evil. The *intent* or *yatser* is first mentioned here in Genesis 6:5 and second

---

[23] BDB Definition: 1) form, framing, purpose, framework יצר

[24] *Evil Within and Without*, Miryam T. Brand.

in Genesis 8:21 where we read again from God, "*I will never again curse the ground because of man, for <u>the intention</u> of man's heart is evil from his youth. Neither will I ever again strike down every living creature as I have done.*" The intention of man heart or mind is evil from his youth. This means that man will always continue to form and shape hurtful and chaotic things in life. Some worse than others.

James White's book [25]*The Potter's Freedom* quotes Genesis 6:5 to try and prove the total depravity of people. The problem with his conclusion is he fails to look at the Hebrew word *yatser* which points back to individuals who are the ones who shape and form evil. God is not the one who created people to be this way but is the result of the fall and the obtaining of knowledge which belongs to God. One other thing James White fails to answer is how Noah was not counted as part of the wicked. Noah was human too, and yet he did not act wickedly as the rest of creation. How did Noah avoid the *yatser* of the wicked heart? Before we continue to answer other Bible verses that

---

[25] *The Potter's Freedom*, James White, pg.79.

James White likes to use to point to men's wicked heart in the Old Testament, let us look at Noah and how he attained and acquired God's grace.

NOAH AND GRACE

Grace, "*A masculine noun meaning favor, grace, acceptance. Meaning an unmerited favor or regard in God's sight.*" This is the most common understanding of the word "grace" in our pulpits today. Every modern preacher I have seen on TV and heard on the radio has given that meaning while preaching. Even in most concordances and lexicons, that meaning is conveyed. But where does that word come from in the Bible? What is the origin of the word "grace" and what was the true meaning and understanding of the word? Before the New Testament was written how did the Jews understand "grace" from the Hebrew Bible? Most Christian believers will be shocked to learn that "grace" did not have the meaning of "unmerited favor" as understood today.

When God was about to destroy the earth by a flood, he spoke to Noah and told him to make an ark and put his family inside of it for safety. God warned Noah and protected him and his family from the flood. But why?

Gen.6:8 ונח מצא חֵן בעיני יהוה ²⁶"*But Noah found favor (grace) in the eyes of YHVH.*"

The word "favor" in Genesis 6:8 is the word *grace* that is used to teach unmerited favor. Genesis 6:8 is the first time we see the word *grace* used in the Hebrew Bible. But there is something in the Hebrew that you cannot see in the English translations. First, let me point out that Noah *found* or as the literal ²⁷Hebrew puts it, *attained/acquired* favor or grace. The Hebrew word *matsa* is best translated as attained or acquired. Noah acquired favor/grace from God. Does that sound like unmerited favor? How did Noah acquire favor or grace?

Gen.6:9 "*These are the generations of Noah. Noah was a righteous man, blameless in his generation. Noah walked with God.*" (ESV)

---

²⁶ The bold Hebrew letters is the word *chen* חֵן for *grace*.

²⁷ BDB Definition: 1) to find, attain to, to acquire. מצא

Noah attained or acquired grace from God because he had a relationship with God. Noah was a truthful man who walked with God. Therefore God instructed him to build an ark for his protection. We also read this in Genesis 7:1,

*"Then YHVH said to Noah, "Go into the ark, you and all your household, for **I have seen that you are righteous before me in this generation.**"*

Noah acted righteously before YHVH and YHVH saw and gave him protection or grace. But what about the word *grace*?

The Hebrew word for grace is חֵן (CheN) with two Hebrew letters, the *Chet* and the *Nun*. In [28]ancient Hebrew, the letters represented a word and a picture. The first letter in the Hebrew word for *grace* represents a fence that surrounds and protects. Therefore, the Hebrew picture for *chet* looks like a fence. And the second Hebrew letter, the *nun*, means life or to propagate, Psalm 72:17, and the Hebrew word picture

---

[28] *Hebrew Word Pictures*, Frank Seekins, pg.169;239

resembles a symbol for life. Both Hebrew letters can be found in the Hebrew Bible as a word by themselves. Now, if we take that same Hebrew word for *grace*, *CheN*, and write it backward, it will spell the Hebrew name for Noah. The *Nun* and the *Chet* combined make the name Noah in English. So, Noah in the eyes of YHVH, like a backward reflection, makes the word grace or favor in Hebrew. Noah (Nun, Chet) attained or acquired grace (Chet, Nun) in the eyes of YHVH. This makes sense in the Hebrew word picture because Noah attained God's protection of his life by building the ark. The ark is a picture of grace, God's protection. This is the very foundation of the word *grace* or *favor* without the meaning of unmerited since Noah attained protection from God by having a personal relationship with him before the flood. The majority of Christians who believe "unmerited favor" teaching try very hard to explain this away because it does not fit their theology of grace. Especially those in the Reform Calvinism movement. [29]John Piper confirms this view

---

[29] *The Justification of God*, second edition, John Piper. An Exegetical and Theological Study of Romans 9:1-23.

in his book *The Justification of God*, pg.82-83.

If we continue to follow the Hebrew word for *grace* in the Old Testament, we will see a pattern develop. In the entire first five books of Moses, the Torah, the word *grace* or *favor* is always preceded by the word "found" which in Hebrew means *attained* or *acquired*. This is also true in the Writings and the Prophets until we get to Psalms and Proverbs. The English Bible translators begin to translate the Hebrew word for grace as graceful, adornment and charm. About 95%+ of the entire Hebrew Bible reads, "...found favor..." or more literally, "...attained/acquired favor/protection..." The Jewish and Hebrew understanding was that an individual could attain God's protection and mercy. The phrase was also understood and used toward kings and men in the Hebrew Old Testament. It was never defined or interpreted as unmerited favor. If one reads merely and follows the Hebrew word throughout the Old Testament, you cannot help but see the pattern. Here are some examples.

Gen.18:3 "*and said, (Abraham) "O Lord, if I have **found favor** in **your sight**, do not pass by your servant."*

Gen.19:19 (Lot speaking) "*Behold, your servant has **found favor** in **your sight**, and you have shown me great kindness in saving my life. But I cannot escape to the hills, lest the disaster overtake me, and I die.*"

Exo.33:12 "*Moses said to the LORD, "See, you say to me, 'Bring up these people,' but you have not let me know whom you will send with me. Yet you have said, 'I know you by name, and you have also **found favor** in **my sight**.'"*

Jdg.6:17 "*So Gideon said to Him, "If now I have **found favor** in **Your sight**, then show me a sign that it is You who speak with me.*"

These are just a few passages that show part of the 95%+ of texts that prove my findings. The Old Testament Hebrew Bible supports that *favor* or *grace* is not grounded in the teaching of unmerited favor. Any person can search out for themselves the passages that are part of the 95%+ and see the pattern of the phrase

"*...found favor in your sight...*" So, what about the New Testament? Does it support the unmerited favor teaching?

NOTE: The word "grace" in Hebrew is never connected with receiving eternal life. In other words, "grace" does not equal eternal life. It is used to convey God's protection and blessing to his people who follow his commandments or Torah. If they do not keep his word, then grace (God's blessing and protection) is removed, and they can be put under God's curse. Also, the Hebrew word "CheN" for *grace* is translated in the Greek LXX as "charin" which is the same as the New Testament Greek word "charis" or "chariti."

As we come to the New Testament, we must remember that all we have, for the most part, are Greek copies and fragments. The Greek is not the same as Hebrew. Greek is an abstract language that comes from Semitic languages. Hebrew is concrete and is based on pictures and words for each letter while Greek does not. With that note, let us look at one of the foundation verse that is used to teach unmerited favor/grace in the

New Testament. It comes from Ephesians 2:8-9, "*For **by grace** you have been saved through faith. And this is not your own doing; it is the gift of God, not a result of works, so that no one may boast.*"

Ephesians 2:8-9 is part of the foundation for "unmerited favor" teaching. But how do we get the word *grace* translated into these verses? It is a body of scholars who come together to decide how to translate the Hebrew and the Greek into English that will be easier to read for the reader. In Ephesians 2:8 we see the word *grace* in the passage. But does that word mean *unmerited favor* in Greek? How is it translated to the rest of the New Testament? The Greek word for *grace* in Ephesians 2:8 is χάρις (charis). The shock to most Christian believers will be that *charis* is not always translated *grace* with the understanding of unmerited favor. In the New American Standard Bible, the Greek word *charis* is translated *gracious work* in [30]2Corinthias, "*So we urged Titus that as he had previously made a beginning, so he would also complete in you this **gracious***

---

[30] NASB 2Corinthians 8:6-7, χάρις for *gracious work* in the Greek.

*work as well. But just as you abound in everything, in faith and utterance and knowledge and in all earnestness and in the love, we inspired in you, see that you abound in this **gracious work** also."*

One translation, the ESV, has "act of grace" while others translate with either *grace* or *work*. In fact, within the New Testament, we find the Greek word being translated in numerous ways. We see the translation of *credit, benefit, blessing, thanks, gratitude, concession*, etc. The Greek word is never used to mean just grace. Why? If this word is supposed to mean "unmerited favor" in connection with eternal life and salvation, then why does it change in meaning when used in other verses? This answer is simple. Men have decided to translate the Greek word into *grace* into the verses they believe it has the meaning of the unmerited favor teaching. Also, the Greek cannot translate the Hebrew word correctly for *grace* in the New Testament. As we have already seen, the Hebrew word is connected with Noah and his name in Hebrew. So, Ephesians 2:8 can be translated as follows, "*For **by His gracious work** you have been saved through faith. And this is not your own doing; it is the gift of God, not a result of* *works (your works), so that no one may boast."*

This translation can efficiently work because Jesus did all the work for us by fulfilling the Torah and dying on the cross for the atonement of sins. We are blessed with eternal life through and by his works and not by ours. Remember, the Old Testament is the foundation for the New Testament and both need to be consistent and in harmony. If we understand that *grace* is a blessing and work from God to us for eternal life, then it fits the consistency of the Old Testament usage as well. Even in Romans, the word grace can be retranslated and still fit perfectly with how we receive eternal life.

Rom.3:23 *"...for all have sinned and fall short of the glory of God, and are justified by his **grace** as a gift, through the redemption that is in Christ Jesus,"*

Rom.3:23 *"...for all have sinned and fall short of the glory of God, and are justified by his **gracious work/blessing** as a gift, through the redemption that is in Christ Jesus,"*

Both passages are true if we understand grace to mean, not unmerited favor, but God's work and blessing in our lives. We are justified by the work of Jesus as a gift to us. But for us to receive this blessing from God through his work through Jesus, we need to have faith and believe in the one who completed the work. Therefore Jesus can be full of grace or blessings and how we can fall from grace or his blessings. Below are more examples of how the Greek word *charis* is translated in most Bibles and others retranslated by me.

Luk.6:32 *"But if you love those who love you, what* **credit** *is that to you? For even sinners love those, who love them."* (English Majority Text Version) See also verse 33-34, *"credit."*

Luk.17:9 *"Does he* **thank** *the servant because he did what was commanded?"* (ESV)

Act.18:27 *"And when he wished to cross to Achaia, the brothers encouraged him and wrote to the disciples to welcome him. When he arrived, he greatly helped those who* *through **grace [His gracious work]** had believed,"* (My translation added)

Rom.1:5 *"Through Christ, God gave me the **special work** of an apostle – to lead people of all nations to believe and obey him. I do all this to honor Christ."* (Easy To Read Version)

Rom.3:24 *"being justified as a gift by His **grace [gracious work]** through the redemption which is in Christ Jesus;"* (NASB-brackets added)

Gal.2:21 *"I do not nullify the **grace [The work/blessing]** of God, for if righteousness were through the law, then Christ died for no purpose."* (ESV-brackets added)

I can continue to post verse after verse showing that if we consider the Greek word *charis* to be understood as gracious work, blessing with God's protection that all still fit the context and the meaning from the Old Testament. In many of the New Testament salutations we see "…grace and peace…" or "The grace of our Lord Jesus…" which is better understood from the Hebrew old Testament greetings of "Blessings…" We should be translating those New Testament verses "…blessings and peace…" and "The blessings of our Lord Jesus…" This fits best when we consider the Jewish understanding of the Hebrew Bible.

The word "grace" in the New Testament has been overused dramatically that it has lost its true meaning which is grounded in Genesis 6:8 and the rest of the Old Testament. The challenge will be to abandon the modern tradition of "unmerited favor" or something for nothing teaching and realize that God grants us eternal life by our faith and trust in him through Jesus the Messiah. In doing so, we receive his blessings and protection in the form of grace and mercy. The teaching of eternal life comes from many New Testament verses with the condition of believing in Jesus as the son of man and as Messiah. In fact, the Gospel of John was written for this very purpose.

Joh.20:31 *"but these have been written so that you may believe that Jesus is the Christ, the Son of God; and that **believing** you may have **life in His name**."* (NASB)

Joh.3:15 "...*that whoever **believes** in him (the son of man) may have **eternal life**.*" (ESV)

Joh.6:40 "*For this is the will of my Father, that everyone who looks on the Son and **believes** in him should have **eternal life**, and I will raise him up on the last day.*" (ESV)

Joh.6:47 "*Truly, truly, I say to you, whoever **believes** has **eternal life**.*" (ESV)

In other parts of the New Testament, we see another connection to eternal life regarding belief and seeking. This does not suggest that we receive eternal life by works. But there is an action on our part of coming to God in trust and faith regarding Jesus. To a Jew, trust and belief in Jesus as Messiah is NOT considered work as some may suppose.

Rom.2:7 "*...to those who by patience in well-doing seek for glory and honor and immortality, he will give **eternal life**;*" (ESV)

In other verses in the New Testament, we see the connection between eternal life and grace being used. Here are a couple of examples found in Romans and one in Titus.

Rom.5:21 "...*so that, as sin reigned in death,* **grace** *[His work/blessing] also might reign through righteousness leading to* **eternal life** *through Jesus Christ our Lord.*" (ESV)

Rom.6:23 "*For the wages of sin is death, but the* **gift** *[The work/blessing] of God is eternal life in Christ Jesus our Lord.*" (English Majority Test Version)

Tit.3:7 "*so that being justified by His* **grace** *[His gracious work] we would be made heirs according to the hope of* **eternal life**." (ESV)

[31]Paul continues his teaching to Timothy regarding eternal life by saying, "*Yet for this reason, I found mercy, so that in me as the foremost, Jesus Christ might demonstrate*

---

[31] 1Timothy 1:16, NASB.

*His perfect patience as an example for those who would **believe in Him for eternal life**."*

I want to make something very clear. I am not saying we as believers in Jesus the Messiah are saved or justified by the works that we do. Eternal life is in Jesus the Son of God, and by believing and trusting in him and the work, he has done for us. In doing so, we receive the blessing and protection of God in the form of grace and mercy which is the true meaning of *grace* in the Bible as a whole. So why is the meaning of *grace* so important? Because of Calvinist and the majority of Christian scholars and believers have a view of unmerited favor as if nobody can attain or acquire God's mercy and favor yet we see in the Hebrew we can through the example of Noah. And that *grace* is not connected with eternal life in the Hebrew Old Testament. In the Greek New Testament, *grace* was connected with eternal life as the work and blessing from God through Yeshua-Jesus. Both the Hebrew and Greek word for *grace* does not have the same meaning when translated or interpreted. Therefore we must rely on the Hebrew meaning and understanding over the Greek when looking at the New Testament.

THE SOVEREIGNTY OF GOD AND MAN

The [32]origin of the word *sovereignty* is not found in the Hebrew Bible. It is a word that has evolved from Late Latin, Middle French to Old English. In translation, the word *sovereignty* has been taken from the Hebrew word *malkut* or in the English, *kingdom*. Sovereignty has taken the place of the word *kingdom* in regards to its meaning of the reign, power, and ruler. So the sovereignty of God is more literally the Kingdom of God. The word "sovereignty" lacks a precise definition in the English language. In the Christian understanding, the sovereignty of God has become to be known as the total control and power of God over his creation. Although God gives the power to rule to man in their kingdoms God is still in control in the heavens to establish or destroy those kingdoms. In Calvinistic theology, they refer to sovereign authority, sovereign power, sovereign control, sovereign causation, sovereign rule, sovereign reign, sovereign plan, sovereign purpose, sovereign

---

[32] Etymology - Oxford Etymological Dictionary of the English Language.

will, sovereign decrees, sovereign determinations, sovereign counsel, sovereign fore-ordination, sovereign grace, sovereign love, etc. These terms used by Calvinists are inventions within the Reform movement itself. This, in part, has lead Reformers to look at God, who creates man under this sovereign rule, as the final authority in all matters including the decision to elect individuals to eternal life while ignoring others who are not of the elect of God. But is God responsible for every action of man's doing or does man have their responsibility toward God? We have already seen a person's intent in forming evil in his heart and mind against God. Therefore, a person is sovereign over his mind and heart to do good or evil. This is the knowledge to decern right from wrong in a god-like manner that was received from eating the tree of discernment.

  We have already looked at the book of Genesis in regards to the fall, sin, grace, and Noah. But there are other and more subtle verses in the Bible that speak of man's intent vs. God's sovereignty. In Exodus 21, just after Moses give the ten commandments from God, we read another command. *"Whoever strikes a man so that he dies shall be put to death. But if he did not lie in wait for him, but God let him fall into his hand, then I will appoint for you a place to which he may flee."* Exod.21:12-13. The first part of this verse makes it clear that the death caused by a person is planned while the second part says literally from the Hebrew, *"...but God caused him to fall into his hand..."* If a man committed the death on his own, then he will be put to death, but if God caused his death by the hand of the man, then God will direct him where to flee. This is based on the [33]Hebrew root word *anah*. This Hebrew word refers to causing or delivering. This *cause* or *happening* will either be by the hand of man or by the hand of God through man. What man sees as an accidental death may be an act of God as expressed in Exodus 21:12-13. When a person acts on his behalf, against God, he will be put to death in accordance with what the Torah teaches. But according to the majority of Calvinist, a person thoughts are always evil continually. In fact, Dr. James White states in his

---

[33] Cause, befall, deliver, happen אנה

[34]book, "*This corruption is internal and complete: every intent of the thoughts of man's heart was only evil continually. This is radical corruption, not mere "sickness."* Although there is some truth to his statement, Dr. White fails to explain how Noah was able to attain God's grace by being righteous before God. Noah walked with God and had a relationship with God before the flood. God did not elect Noah for no reason. God saw Noah as being righteous and honorable before him. It was Noah's actions that God saw before the flood. After the second fall of man in Genesis 6:1-7 there was nobody who walked with God but Noah. Noah was the last of the righteous. The context of Genesis 6 does not fit with Dr. Whites interpretation as a general statement of corruption with man as if nobody was or could be righteous before God. The *every* as Dr. White illustrates does not include Noah. Immediately after Dr. White fails to explain the acts of Noah, he then moves to Jeremiah 13:23 for more proof of a person's inability to do good.

---

[34] *The Potter's Freedom*; James R. White, page 79.

In Dr. White's [35]book on page 80, he quotes Jeremiah 13:23 as follows, "*Can the Ethiopian change his skin Or the leopard his spots? Then you also can do good Who are accustomed to doing evil.*" (NASB). Dr. White then goes on to explain, "*Just as a person cannot change the color of their skin, or the leopard its spots, so the one who practices evil cannot break the bondage of sin and start doing good.*" Dr. White's explanation is deeply flawed when we look at the context and the Hebrew of Jeremiah 13. We can see the context in verse 22 where Jeremiah records, "*And if you say in your heart, 'Why have these things come upon me?' it is for the greatness of your iniquity that your skirts are lifted up, and you suffer violence.*" (ESV). Judah is the context as a nation who has rebelled against God and will be scattered and exiled from their land. This is not talking about individuals in relation to God. The Hebrew shows not "who practices evil" but who as a nation "who was [36]taught or learned evil." The nation Judah for so long has adopted evil that they can no longer stop doing evil and change to do good.

---

[35] *The Potter's Freedom*, James R. White.

[36] *Strong's*-instructed: - accustomed, disciple, learned, taught, used. למד

Evil had become part of their persona as a nation. Dr. White assumes the evil was already part of their lives individually and they can never change from it. Unfortunately, this is not the case based on the context and the Hebrew behind Jeremiah 13. Dr. White randomly pulls verses out of the Bible to try and show that a person is always evil while ignoring the context or the language. Dr. White does this again on the same page of his [37]book when he quotes Jeremiah 17:9. *"The heart is deceitful above all things, and desperately sick; who can understand it?"* Dr. White tries to explain this verse in the same way as the other Jeremiah passage. Once again, the context is Judah from verse 1 and the sin they have committed against God. The verses leading up to 9 shows another understanding from [38]Jeremiah. *"Thus says the LORD: "Cursed is the man who trusts in man and makes flesh his strength, whose heart turns away from the LORD... "Blessed is the man who trusts in the LORD, whose trust is the LORD."* Jeremiah 17:9 is not a decree statement by Jeremiah but a cry out to God in the form

---

[37] *The Potter's Freedom*, James R. White, page 80.

[38] Jeremiah 17:5;7 (ESV)

of a question that only God can answer in verse 10. Man's heart has turned away from God which demonstrates that it was not *always* deceitful and sick as Dr. White would like you to believe. The man who trusts in the LORD is blessed according to Jeremiah 17:7. Dr. White's general statement to prove that man is *always* wicked and sinful does not hold water when we look at the context of Jeremiah. Unfortunately Dr. White does this with Psalm 51:5 and Psalm 58:3 on the same page in his [39]book. David in Psalm 51:5 cries out that he was brought forth to blame and guilt while conceived in sin. While this is all true, by David, in the sense that we all are guilty and conceived in sin. Remember, the sting of death is sin. The very fact that we all are dying is proof of sin and guilt in all our lives. Nobody can be blameless while we are dying in this flesh. It appears that the majority of Reformers think that sin is a living entity separate from individuals. From the beginning God told Cane that he could master sin, referring to his mind and discernment of good and evil. We sin based on our decisions we make

---

[39] *The Potter's Freedom*, James R. White, page 80.

against God.

We all have the ability to decern right from wrong. If we choose to be our own sovereign king, then we will fail every time. *"Blessed is the man who trusts in the LORD, whose trust is the LORD."* Jeremiah 17:7.

CHOOSE LIFE...

The teaching that people have the ability to come to God freely without God first choosing them is clear in the Old Testament Hebrew Bible and within Judaism itself. God has the power over his creation, and his plan will not fail but people, because of their god-like discernment of good and evil, have their own plans with God or without God. With God, we completely surrender our lives to him and his will for us in this life. Without God, we live under the curse of God in this life and the life to come. God through Moses warned his people in Deut.30:19, "*I call heaven and earth to witness against you today, that I have set before you life and death, blessing and curse. Therefore choose life, that you and your offspring may live, loving the LORD your God, obeying his voice and holding fast to him, for he is your life and length of days, that you may dwell in the land that the LORD swore to your fathers, to Abraham, to Isaac, and to Jacob, to give them.*" This passage in Deuteronomy 30 is the foundation for the rest of the Hebrew Bible and the New Testament. God warns the Hebrews concerning how they should live. If they want to live a long a blessed life, then they need to obey God and listen to his voice. If they do not obey his voice, then the curses of God will fall on them and death will shorten their days. The choice of life or death belongs to God's people. They have the power to choose God's blessings or curses upon themselves. You will see this all throughout the Old Testament where God continues to warn the Jews to return to him or face exile and death.

    The Hebrew word for [40]*choose* is the same word used to describe how God chose his people and delivered them out of Egypt. *"And because he loved your fathers and <u>chose</u> their offspring after them and brought you out of Egypt with his own presence, by his great power,..."* Deut.4:37. Again God uses this word, *"For you are a people holy to the LORD your God. The LORD, your God, has <u>chosen</u> you to be a people for his treasured possession, out of all the peoples who are on the face of the earth."* Deut.7:6. ESV. The word used to describe his people is a *chosen* people of God. This word is also used in the New Testament and is translated from the Greek as *elect*. Again we read how God has chosen his people. *"Blessed*

---

[40] **NASEC-a** prim. root; to choose: — choice בָּחַר

is the nation whose God is the LORD, the people whom he has <u>chosen</u> as his heritage!" But when God's people do not choose God for his blessing, we read, "*Then they will call upon me, but I will not answer; they will seek me diligently but will not find me. Because they hated knowledge and did not <u>choose</u> the fear of the LORD,...*" Proverbs 1:28-29. God again warns, "*Do not envy a man of violence and <u>do not choose</u> any of his ways,...*" Proverbs. 3:31. Why does God warn his people not to choose evil or wickedness? God will punish his people for rebelling against him. A shortened life is promised to those who live against God. Once again, God's people in the Old Testament have a choice based on their knowledge and discernment of good and evil. The people of God are not depraved and only wicked as Calvinist would have you believe. They have a choice to serve God and receive his blessings or to disobey his voice and face the curses of God ending in death. The vast majority of texts that Calvinist use to try and prove total human depravity are the same texts that show God speaking to his people regarding judgment because of their transgression. The texts are not universal to all people like the nations. They are inclusive to his people. There are times when God is speaking to the nations in regards to seeking him. Is it possible to seek God from among the nations?

There is a distinction within the Bible regarding seeking God from among the wicked and seeking God earnestly with the heart. We see that those who are acting wicked and choosing to do evil will not seek God. We read in Psalms, *"For the wicked boasts of the desires of his soul, and the one greedy for gain curses and renounces the LORD. In the pride of his face, the wicked does not seek him; all his thoughts are, "There is no God."* Psalms 10:3-4. The literal Hebrew explains that it is the guilty, the one who is against God who boasts of the desires of his life. He blesses and blasphemes the LORD, and the wicked do not seek God. All his thoughts are "There is no God" meaning there is no judgment for him. Why would an atheist bless and curse God if he doesn't believe in him? The wicked men are not claiming to be an atheist but are claiming to be outside of God's judgment and power. We see this same understanding in Psalms 14:1-7. It is the senseless or foolish ones who say there is no God or judgment from God. The context is Israel who has turned away from God. They do not seek God nor do they do any good. We will see in the New Testament how [41]Paul quotes Psalms 14 to show how both Greeks and Jews are under sin and guilty based on their wickedness. They will not seek God or do good. They do not fear God, and they shed innocent blood. But can the wicked turn back to God? *"Let them turn back because of their shame who say, 'Aha, Aha!' May all who seek you rejoice and be glad in you! May those who love your salvation say evermore, 'God is great!'"* Psalms 70:3-4. The wicked can turn back to God and seek after him and declare, "God is great!" Let us not forget that God speaks collectively to Israel, Judah and sometimes to the nations. *"Seek good and not evil, that you may live;"* Amos 5:14.

---

[41] Romans 3:1-18

GOD IS IN CONTROL

This next part is taken from my book, *The First Satan; Understanding Satans, Devils, and Demons*. I added this portion to show that God in the Old Testament and the New Testament allows and causes good and bad things to happen to individuals. He can be a satan to Balaam, Numbers 22:22;32. He can be a satan to king David, 2Sam.24:1 and 1Chron.21:1. God sends evil spirits against nations to fight against each other, Judges 9:23. God sends evil spirits to torment and possesses individuals like Saul, 1Samuel 16:14-16;23;18:10;19:9. We also see God sending lying spirits to false prophets to cause them to lie, 1Kings 22:15-23. In all these cases God responded to the sin of the individual by being or sending spirits of calamity and torment. But God still says, "*Seek good, and not evil, that you may live; and so the LORD, the God of hosts, will be with you, as you have said.*" Amos 5:14.

In this section, we will be looking at the numerous Bible verses that state *clearly* that God is in control of everything that happens. He is even the one who creates good in the world, and he is also the one who creates chaos in the world too. God allows certain things to happen to his children whether good or bad. This is what we find in the book of Job who was righteous and blameless. Yet, God permitted the adversary Satan to take away Job's family and even to strike him physically. God gave the adversary the power over fire, the winds, and the air to strike Job. God even gave Satan power over nations to strike Job, Job 1:12-19. In the end, Job knew who was responsible for all that he went through. *"I know that you can do all things and that no purpose of yours can be thwarted…and they consoled him and comforted him for all the adversities that the YHVH had brought on him."* Job 42:2;11. The purpose of God was made known to Job at the end, and it was understood that God himself brought all the adversities through Satan onto Job.

God himself takes credit for everything that happens good or bad, *"That men may know from the rising to the setting of the sun That there is no one besides Me. I am the LORD, and there is no other, The One forming light and creating darkness, Causing well-being and creating calamity; I am YHVH who does all these."* Isaiah 45:6-7. He is the one who creates calamity or as some translations say, *"...creating evil;"* In Proverbs 16:4 we read, *"YHVH has made everything for its purpose, even the wicked for the day of trouble."* Everything God does has a purpose. There will be times when we do not know what that purpose is even in times of trouble. Like Job, we must continue to look toward God for our strength and courage. *"Our God is in the heavens; he does all that he pleases."* Psalm 115:3. *"In his hand is the life of every living thing and the breath of all mankind."* Job 12:10. God is the source of life and death. We are in his hands, and nothing can go against his will. It is easy to blame others for what we go through. We can't say it is Satan or the devil who is causing this pain or suffering when it is God who is allowing us to suffer. We see this with the apostles who are told they will go through trial and tribulation for the name of Jesus. Jesus tells Paul he will suffer greatly for him as well. In times of trials and suffering is when we should come to God for comfort and peace. Paul tells us in Philippians 4:6-7, *"...do not be anxious about anything, but in everything by prayer and supplication with thanksgiving let your requests be made known to God. And the peace of God, which surpasses all understanding, will guard your hearts and your minds in Messiah Jesus."* We must come to God to receive our peace and understanding.

Even Paul understands when he was suffering great persecution by his brethren, it was a messenger of Satan who sent to him to keep him from boasting about himself. *"So to keep me from becoming conceited because of the surpassing greatness of the revelations, a thorn was given me in the flesh, a messenger of Satan to harass me, to keep me from becoming conceited."* 2Corinthians 12:7. Three times he prayed the suffering to removed, but God said to him, *"'My grace is sufficient for you, for my power is made perfect in weakness.'"* The Bible does not always give us the answer as to why we must suffer.

Let us remember the words of King Nebuchadnezzar who was suffering at the hands of God when he said, *"But at the end of that period, I, Nebuchadnezzar, raised my eyes toward heaven and my reason returned to me, and I blessed the Most High and praised and honored Him who lives forever; For His dominion is an everlasting dominion, And His kingdom endures from generation to generation.* "*All the inhabitants of the earth are accounted as nothing, But He does according to His will in the host of heaven And among the inhabitants of earth; And no one can ward off His hand Or say to Him, 'What have You done?'*" Why did Nebuchadnezzar finally realize this? Daniel told him earlier that, "*...seven periods of time will pass over you until you recognize that the Most High is ruler over the realm of mankind and bestows it on whomever He wishes.*" Daniel 4:34;25. The King finally realized who is really in control and who rules over humanity and creation. God will give to whom he wishes and will allow acts of violence and good in the world for his purpose and will. God uses his heavenly armies and spirits of chaos to do his will. No independent evil spirits or demons are running around tormenting people without the permission of God who grants them to do so. In times of trouble, we must come before God on our face and ask him for mercy and grace. His protection of us is sufficient. If we must suffer then, we must continue to sing praise to him who is allowing it. Do not let tradition continue to influence you into believing that devils and demons are looking to attack you without cause. Satans, devils, and demons are all under God's control, and he will direct them to do his will according to his purpose, not ours. *"Yours, YHVH, is the greatness and the power and the glory and the victory and the majesty, for all that is in the heavens and on the earth is yours. Yours is the kingdom, O YHVH, and you are exalted as head above all. Both riches and honor come from you, and you rule over all. In your hand are power and might, and in your hand, it is to make great and to give strength to all. And now we thank you, our God, and praise your glorious name."* 2Chronicles 29:11-13. Amen and amen!

The understanding that God is in control does not take away from the fact that individuals are accountable for their actions against God. We can [42]seek good and not evil. We can [43]gain control of sin which is crouching at the door, Genesis 4:7. The idea that no one can do good or seek God with an honest heart is false and misleading. We know that God's plan for humanity will be fulfilled but along the way people can and will try to fulfill their plans outside of God.

---

[42] Amos 5:14

[43] NASEC- a prim. root; to rule, have dominion, reign, gain control. מָשַׁל

2nd TEMPLE PERIOD AND THE NEW TESTAMENT

When we come to the New Testament for understanding or teaching, we must first be grounded in the Old Testament. The foundation for the New Testament is the Hebrew Bible referred to as the Old Testament. If you only are grounded in the New Testament, then you will misapply and misinterpret the New Testament texts. Jews who followed Yeshua-Jesus wrote the New Testament. We know with certainty that Yeshua-Jesus spoke and taught his disciples in the [44]Hebrew language. The Greek New Testament is then a translation of what Yeshua-Jesus taught and said to his disciples. Whether you believe that the New Testament was written originally in Greek, it is still a translation from the Hebrew spoken by Yeshua-Jesus to his disciples. We must come to the New Testament with [45]Hebrew lenses called the Hebrew Scriptures. So the question we must answer is, "Did the 1st century Jews believe and teach a Reform doctrine of some kind

---

[44] *The Language Environment of First Century Judaea*, volume two. Brill.

[45] *The Gospels in First Century Judaea*, Brill.

in regards to total depravity and special election?" As we already showed, the Hebrew Scriptures do not support such a view. So what about the New Testament and early Jewish sources?

Before we look at the New Testament, we will look at some Jewish sources discovered among the Dead Sea Scroll. The Damascus Document Scroll was discovered in Cave 4 at Qumran. According to [46]Dr. Miryam T. Brand, "...*the Damascus Document reflects the author's view of sin and human agency. The key terms that indicate the human inclination to sin are the 'will' of the actors and 'the stubbornness of their heart.'*" She goes on to say, "*The designation of a person's 'will' as a cause of sin is evident from the beginning of history. The author relates Abraham, as a 'lover' of God, kept the commandments of God and <u>did not choose</u> the <u>will fo his spirit</u>.*" [47]Dr. Brand goes on to conclude based on the Damascus Documents that, "*Abraham <u>chose to ignore his own will</u>, which would naturally lead him to sin.*" The Damascus Document appears to agree with the Hebrew Scriptures about

---

[46] *Evil Within and Without*, Miryam T. Brand, page 78. CD III.2-12a

[47] Evil Within and Without, Miryam T Brand, page 79. CD III.2-3a

sinners who abandoned God's covenant and commandments because they chose to follow their own sinful desires.

Dr. Miryam Brand is not a believer in Yeshua-Jesus, so she has no connection to Christian beliefs regarding Calvinism or Arminianism. She is an Orthodox Jewish believer, an academic scholar, and an expert in 2nd Temple texts.

Another passage in the Damascus Document speaks of Ezekiel 14:3. *"Son of man, these men have taken their idols into their hearts, and set the stumbling block of their iniquity before their faces. Should I indeed let myself be consulted by them?"* [48]Dr. Brand says, *"These passages of the Damascus Document indicate the both those who successfully refrain from sin, that is, those who choose God's commandments and reject their own will, and those who return to sin by 'placing idols' on their hearts, act out of choice...This freedom underlies all human's complete responsibility for their own sins, and for any punishment that may result from it."* Based on Dr. Brand's study of the Damascus Document we can see how the

---

[48] Evile Within and Without, Miryam T. Brand, page 82 CD XX.9-10

understanding of certain Hebrew texts in the Old Testament was viewed. Men have the freedom to choose to obey God and his commandments or to reject them and live according to their own will and sinful desires or inclination. Once again this is consistent with the Hebrew Scriptures that we have already studied earlier. Though there are points within the Damascus Document regarding predestination and foreknowledge, it does not support the view of Calvinism or Reform theology regarding eternal life through a selection of the elect. The view in the document shows how God knew their actions of the wicked before they were created. Based on God's foreknowledge he withholds the possibility of choice because he knows their actions before they do them. In other words, because God knows that a wicked person will never return or seek God, God will use them for his will and glory. We see this in Exodus regarding Pharaoh. God tells Moses that the king of Egypt will not allow them to leave Egypt unless under strong and mighty hand. *"But I know that the king of Egypt will not let you go unless compelled by a mighty hand. So I will stretch out my hand and strike Egypt with all the wonders that I will do in it; after that, he will let you go."* Exodus 3:19-20. God knows that Pharaoh will not let the Hebrews go before Moses even gets to Egypt. And God also knew that only after he strikes Egypt with his power that the king will then let them go free. God also told Moses that he would "hold back" Pharaoh's choice to let them go until all his wonders are complete, Exodus 4:21. God did not cause or create Pharaoh to be a wicked king by holding back his choice to let the Hebrews free. God already knew Pharaoh's heart and mind and used him to show his power against his false gods and idols. God demonstrated his foreknowledge and predestination of Pharaoh by telling Moses what will happen and what he will do to Pharaoh before he lets them go free. This is consistent with the Damascus Document and the Hebrew Scriptures.

In Dr. Brand's book, *Evil Within and Without*, She builds the case of moral choice on the Hebrew word *yeser* in Genesis 6:5 and 8:21. From the book of Ben Sir [49]Dr. Brand makes this comment, *"The result is that the*

---

[49] Evil Within and Without, Dr. Mirym T. Brand, page 101.

yeser as it appears in Sir 15:14 is a neutral capacity that enables the human being to make a moral choice. In other words, the yeser in 15:14 reflects the moral choice of the human being, and in keeping with biblical use, denotes human character...this choice has always been a human capability." This conclusion from Dr. Brand of Ben Sir is in direct contradiction to Reform theology within Calvinism. This should be of no surprise since Reform theology is a much later form of doctrine that is being forced into the Hebrew Bible and the New Testament.

Dr. Brand continues through the writings of 4 Ezra, 2 Baruch, and Philo of Alexandria coming to the same conclusions of moral choice being part of human beings. In other words, people have a choice between right and wrong, good and evil because they have obtained the knowledge of God with regards to decerning good and evil for themselves.

The New Testament

As we start to look in the New Testament, we need to understand the beliefs within the Jewish leaders called Pharisees. The apostle Paul was trained by the grandson of Hillel who was one of the greatest sages of Judaism. Paul was a Pharisee and continued to be a Pharisee after he became a believer in Yeshua-Jesus. [50]Paul said, *"Brethren, I am a Pharisee, the son of a Pharisee..."* while he was on trial and speaking to Sadducees and Pharisees. So the question we must ask is, *"What were the central beliefs about 'free will' and the sovereignty of God.?"* The Calvinist believe their understanding of sin and depravity is consistent with Paul. But do we have any writings that we can look at during the 1st century that reflect the views of the Pharisees?

Titus Flavius Josephus was a first-century Romano-Jewish scholar, historian, and hagiographer, who was born in Jerusalem then part of Roman Judea to a father of priestly descent and a mother who claimed royal ancestry. His views of the Pharisees and their beliefs regarding the sovereignty of God and free will is worth noticing. According to Josephus the Pharisees held to a certain view that made it impossible for either free will or the sovereignty of God to cancel

---

[50] Acts 23:6

out the other. [51]*"They assert that everything is accomplished by faith. They do not, however, deprive the human will of spontaneity, it having pleased God that there should be a mixture, and that to the will of fate should be added the human will with its virtue or baseness."* [52]Josephus concludes with God having sovereignty over his creation, but men can act virtuously or viciously on their own. This mixture of sovereignty and freedom of choice is what we see in the Hebrew Old Testament. Even in the Jewish [53]Mishnah, we read, *"all is foreseen, but freedom of choice is given."*

Before we look at Paul's writings, we need first to respond to Dr. White's chapter in his book, *The Potter's Freedom,* titled "[54]Jesus Teaches 'Extreme Calvinism.' Dr. White focuses on the gospel of John to show that 1500 years before Calvin, Jesus was teaching that man is "so dead" that he is incapable of coming to Christ on his own. Dr. White refers to irresistible grace

---

[51] *Josephus*, Ant.18.1.3

[52] *Josephus*. Antiq.18. 1. 3:13

[53] *Aboth* 2:16

[54] *The Potter's Freedom*, chapter 7 page 153.

on the elect (not on the willing) in regards to salvation. As we have already seen earlier in the book, "grace" has been misunderstood and mistranslated in the New Testament. Dr. White quotes John 6 37-40 for proof of Jesus teaching irresistible grace in Calvinism. The first thing I must point out is how we look at the gospels. The gospels are historical narratives. They are recording the life and teachings of Yeshua-Jesus before his death. He focuses on bringing the good news of the kingdom to the [55]lost sheep of the house of Israel. Yeshua-Jesus declares to his disciple to not go among the Gentiles or the Samaritans. I say this because Dr. White is using the gospel of John as universal teaching and ignoring the context of the historical setting, the audience and the use of the Hebrew Old Testament by Yeshua-Jesus.

John 6:37-45

As we look at the context of John 6:37-40 we see that Yeshua-Jesus arrives in Capernaum. The people were seeking him after arriving in Capernaum in small

---

[55] Matthew 10:5-6 ESV

boats. Yeshua-Jesus was in the synagogue in Capernaum when the people found him. When the people asked Yeshua-Jesus when he arrived in Capernaum Yeshua-Jesus tells them, [56]*"Truly, truly, I say to you, you are seeking me, not because you saw signs, but because you ate your fill of the loaves."* The people were seeking Yeshua-Jesus because he feeds them and not because of his miracles. Yeshua-Jesus then tells them not to work for food that parishes but to work for the food which endures to eternal life which is the Son of Man who will give it to them. Yeshua-Jesus is telling them how to receive eternal life. The people then ask Yeshua-Jesus, [57]*"What must we do, to be doing the works of God?"* The response of the people is referring to how they can work and receive eternal life which is salvation. Yeshua-Jesus sets the record straight by answering, [58]*"This is the work of God, that you believe in him whom he has sent."* In other words, Yeshua-Jesus tells them that if they want to do the works of God for

---

[56] John 6:26 ESV

[57] John 6:28 ESV

[58] John 6:29 ESV

eternal life then believe in him who God sent. That is the work needed for salvation, believe him, Yeshua-Jesus. Yeshua-Jesus did not tell them that the works of God are only for those who are chosen or elected. Then the people, they want to see a sign so that they can believe in him.

Yeshua-Jesus continues to teach the people the following, [59]*"I am the bread of life; whoever comes to me shall not hunger, and whoever believes in me shall never thirst. But I said to you that you have seen me and yet do not believe."* The first thing we need to notice from the Greek is the change from a singular person to plural persons. In the Greek, it is the individual who comes and believes in Yeshua-Jesus who will never thirst which is referring to eternal life and salvation. And then Yeshua-Jesus says in the second person plural "you all" have seen me and yet "you all" do not believe. Immediately Yeshua-Jesus says right after, [60]*"All that the Father gives me will come to me, and whoever comes to me I will never cast out."* The "All" that Yeshua-

---

[59] John 6:35-36 ESV

[60] John 6:37

Jesus is referring to are those standing in front of him. He is not referring to all human being throughout time. Everyone who continues to come to Yeshua-Jesus through the Father will not be cast out. Yeshua-Jesus confirms who he is speaking about in verse 40, *"For this is the will of my Father, that everyone who looks on the Son and believes in him should have eternal life, and I will raise him up on the last day."* ESV. The Greek says it is the ones "beholding the Son" and who believes in him will have eternal life. Once again Yeshua-Jesus is speaking to the people in the synagogue standing before him and not *everyone,* present, and future. To further prove that Yeshua-Jesus is not talking about some universal elect that the Father gives to the Son for eternal life we need to look at verse 44 and 45.

After the Jews finish grumbling about what Yeshua-Jesus says about himself being the bread of life who came down from heaven, Yeshua-Jesus says, *"No one can come to me unless the Father who sent me draws him. And I will raise him up on the last day. It is written in the Prophets, 'And they will all be taught by God.' Everyone who has heard and learned from the Father comes to me."* ESV. The majority of Calvinist stop reading at verse 44 and ignore verse 45 which is a quote from the Hebrew Scriptures and explains how and who the Father draws. The phrase "*...in the Prophets,*" in verse 45 can be read as singular or plural. The Ethiopic text reads "*...in the book of the Prophets,*" while the Syriac reads "*...in the Prophet,*" One thing is for certain, Yeshua-Jesus is referring to Isaiah 54:13 where he says, "*All your children shall be taught by the LORD, and great shall be the peace of your children.*" ESV. And could also be referring to a Messianic passage in Micah 4:2, "*and many nations shall come, and say: 'Come, let us go up to the mountain of the LORD, to the house of the God of Jacob, that he may teach us his ways and that we may walk in his paths.' For out of Zion shall go forth the Torah, and the Word of the LORD from Jerusalem.*" In Isaiah and Micah, God is speaking to Israel who is being punished for their sins against him. But in the days of the Messiah, he promises them that their children will be discipled or be disciples by or of the LORD. What Yeshua-Jesus is trying to tell the Jews is that only those who are true disciples of the LORD will be lead by the Father to the Son. Those disciples were taught and learned by the Father according to Yeshua-Jesus. The Aramaic translation of Isaiah also confirms this by saying, "*all your children shall learn in the Torah of the LORD.*" This passage is only referring to Jews and not to the nations universally as Dr. White would have you believe. The [61]Jews themselves acknowledge the prophecy belongs to the times of the Messiah and not to the nations, [62]"*They are truly taught of God from whom prophecy comes, which does not to all the world, but to Israel only, of whom it is written, 'and all thy children are taught of God'.*" So Yeshua-Jesus is speaking in the present while standing before the Jews and not speaking of some future universal salvation of some elect people. The context, historical setting, the Jewish sources, and the Hebrew Scriptures do not allow for Dr. White's interpretation of John 6:37-45.

John 12:27-33

Another text in John that is discussed among Calvinist and non-Calvinist is John 12:27-33. The context starts in verse 20 of John 12, "*Now among those*

---

[61] John 6:45, *John Gill NT Commentary*; Shemot Rabba, sect.15.fol.102.4. Kimichi in loc.

[62] John 6:45, *John Gill NT Commentary*, Zohar in Exod. fol. 70. 1.

who went up to worship at the feast were some Greeks." ESV. According to [63]Dr. White, the Greeks were non-Jew, Gentiles. Other scholars believe John is speaking about Greek-speaking Jews among the dispersion. This idea of Greek-speaking Jews come from John 7:35 where we read, *"The Jews said to one another, "Where does this man intend to go that we will not find him? Does he intend to go to the Dispersion among the Greeks and teach the Greeks?"* The Jews thought that Yeshua-Jesus would leave them and go to the Greek-speaking Jews and teach them. We know with certainty Yeshua-Jesus forbid his disciples to preach the gospel to Gentiles or the nations including the Samaritans, Matthew 10:5. They were to only preach to the lost sheep of the house of Israel or [64]Jacob which includes lost tribes that were scattered and exiled by God. The "Greeks" did not only refer to Gentiles or non-Jews which would have been [65]forbidden by the Yehsua-Jesus until he was raised from the dead. Also, there is no way that

---

[63] The Potter's Freedom, James R. White, page 163.

[64] Genesis 49:1-28

[65] Matthew 10:5; after his resurrection, Acts 10:28;45, 11:1

uncircumcised Greeks and or Gentiles would go up to worship at a Jewish feast. Others might argue that they were proselytes, but that is not likely given the above explanation for Greek-speaking Jews. Proselytes are mentioned by name in Acts 13:43. This explanation of Greek-speaking Jews corrects Dr. White's misunderstanding of John 12, and its context which he affirms is an [66]important turn of events.

So when we come to the key verse in John 12, *"And I, when I am lifted up from the land, will draw all people to myself..."* we can see that what Yeshua-Jesus was trying to say with regards to *"...draw all to myself."* In the Greek "men" is not in the passage. One [67]commentary says, *"Beza's most ancient copy, and some others, and the Vulgate Latin version read παντα, 'all things'; and by 'all' are meant, all the elect of God, all the children of God, 'that were scattered abroad'; the Persic version reads, 'I will draw my friends to me.'"* The "scattered abroad" must be about the exiled Jews who are also the elect of God along with the Jews in Jerusalem. We can see this

---

[66] The Potter's Freedom, James R. White, page 163.

[67] *John Gill's NT Commentary*, John 12:32.

"drawing" or "⁶⁸leading" by Yeshua-Jesus being fulfilled in Acts 2:5-11. Again, the context of John 12:20-32 cannot be referring to non-Jews or Gentiles based on Peter's testimony in ⁶⁹Acts 10 as mentioned earlier. The gospel of John is a historical narrative and must be read and interpreted as such. It should not be used to affirm someone's doctrine or theology without consulting the Hebrew Scriptures for support. If Yeshua-Jesus says "you" he is not speaking to you, the reader. This is typically ignored by Calvinist and sometimes by non-Calvinist too.

In brief, Calvinist will use other passages like 1Corinthians 1:24 to try and show Jews and Greeks are elected by God by using a word like "called" to support their view. But they fail to consider the true meaning of the verse and word from the Greek in both the Old Testament, the ⁷⁰LXX, and the New Testament. Paul says, "...*but to those who are called, both Jews and Greeks,*

---

[68] Thayer's Difinition, ἑλκύω / ἕλκω. to draw by inward power, lead, impel.

[69] Acts 10:28;45, 11:1.

[70] LXX or 70 is the Greek translation of the Hebrew Old Testament call the Septuagint.

Christ the power of God and the wisdom of God." ESV. According to *The Complete Word Study Dictionary*, κλητός-klētós "called" was used to designate those invited to a banquet (Sept.: 1Ki_1:41, 1Ki_1:49). So Paul is saying those who are invited are both Jews and Greeks. That does not sound like a chosen elect as Calvinist whould believe. If you are invited to a wedding, do you have the choice to go or not to go? Yes, of course you have a choice. Paul continues with, *"For consider your calling* (invitation)*, brothers: not many of you were wise according to worldly standards, not many were powerful, not many were of noble birth."* The Greek translation uses the same root word for "called" from verse 24. Now, the Greek word can be translated as "called" but the context will determine the translation to be used.

Ephesians 1:1-11 and Romans 7-11

I am starting with Ephesians before Romans to show a similar word pattern with "predestination," "chose us," and "adoption," that is used in Romans after chapter 7. This will guide us into Romans which will be our longest chapter. In Ephesians, we will continue to see how Calvinist use terms like "us" and "we" as a universal application as if Paul is speaking to you the reader. This is the same error that Dr. White commits while interpreting John 6 and 12. Again he will ignore the historical context, setting, Jewish sources, and the Hebrew Scriptures.

Before we begin to exegete Ephesian 1-11, we need to look at the book Acts for the background and history of the Ephesians. When Paul came to Ephesus, he was already going to the synagogues reasoning with Jews about Yeshua-Jesus as Messiah. We read his arrival to Ephesus in Acts 18:19. He went to the synagogue at Ephesus and reasoned with the Jews for a short time. When he left another Jew came to Ephesus named [71]Apollos who was strong in the Scriptures. He also went to the [72]synagogue, and in public, he would refute the Jews showing that Yeshua-Jesus is the Messiah. Paul returns to Ephesus and goes back to the synagogue for three months speaking about the

---

[71] Acts 18:24

[72] Acts 19:26;28

kingdom of God. When some of the Jews began to speak against Paul and *The Way*, he took the disciples and went to the school of Tyrannus for two years. Those who [73]heard the Word of the Lord were both Jews and Greeks who lived in Ephesus. Those Greeks are more likely part of the uncircumcised non-Jews based on Ephesians 2:11. This takes us back to Ephesians 1:3-11 to look at the context of Jews and Greeks being mentioned in the letter from Paul.

According to Dr. White in his book, [74]The Potter's Freedom, he assumes that Ephesians 1:3-11 is speaking to both Jews and Gentile as Christians by the use of "us" in the text and that it is the formula for how God chooses his elect for salvation. This can further from the truth in understanding the context, the Hebrew Scriptures and historical background. Dr. White makes the classic mistake of assuming that everything written in the Bible is to himself, the reader, because he reads "you" or "us" in the text.

---

[73] Acts 19:10;17

[74] The Potter's Freedom, James R. White, page 175-181

In Ephesians 1:3 we read the opening of Jewish prayer or benediction by Paul, "*Blessed be the God and Father of our Lord Jesus Christ,*" ESV. This prayer is what Jews call a standing prayer or "Amidah." Typically, the first part of the prayer by Jews is as follows, "*Praised be you, Lord, our God, and God of our fathers, God of Abraham, God of Isaac and God of Jacob...*" Even the next part of Ephesians, "*even as <u>he chose us</u> in him before the foundation of the world, that we should be holy and blameless before him...*" has the understanding of choosing Israel and the Jews in the Amidah prayer, "*Praised be you, Adonai, who has <u>chosen your people Israel</u> in love.*" Remember, Paul is a Jewish Pharisee who was trained as a Jew and not a Greek or Gentile. In the Hebrew Scriptures of the Old Testament, we see this type of language regarding "chose" or "choose" used for Israel and the Jewish people, NOT the Gentiles or nations.

"*For you are a people holy to the LORD your God. The LORD your God has <u>chosen you</u> to be a people for his treasured possession, out of all the peoples who are on the face of the earth.*" Deut. 7:6 ESV.

"For the LORD has <u>chosen Jacob</u> for himself, <u>Israel</u> as his possession." Psalm 135:4 ESV

"But you, Israel, my servant, Jacob, whom <u>I have chosen</u>, the offspring of Abraham, my friend;" Isaiah 41:8 ESV

This type of language is what we also find in the New Testament, and the mind of Paul who was trained in the Hebrew Scriptures. In fact, Paul uses this same type of wording in Romans 11:7 when he is speaking about Israel, *"What then? What <u>Israel is seeking</u>, it has not obtained, but those <u>who were chosen</u> obtained it, and the rest were hardened."* We will see later that Paul is not speaking about salvation but a remnant of believers among Israel.

The next passage in Ephesians 1 is verse 5, *"he predestined us for adoption to himself as sons through Jesus Christ, according to the purpose of his will,"* ESV. We do not need to look to the Old Testament to find out who Paul is speaking to in this passage. In Romans 10 and 11 we find our answers. Paul starts in Romans 7:1 to let the reader know who he is now going to be referring to until Romans 11:13. The audience, according to Paul, is those who know the Torah or Law. Who would that be? Paul would be referring to the Jews and who God intrusted the very [75]oracles of his word. The change of reader does not happen until Romans 11:13 where then Paul says, "*Now I am speaking to you Gentiles. Inasmuch then as I am an apostle to the Gentiles,*" ESV. So from Romans 7 to 11:13, we should interpret the passages as speaking to the Jews and not the Gentiles. This cannot be ignored. So when we read Romans 8:29 which says, "*For those whom he foreknew he also predestined to be conformed to the image of his Son, in order that he might be the firstborn among many brothers.*" ESV, we need to ask ourselves, "Who did God ' foreknow" that he 'predestined'?" We find the answer from Paul in Romans 11:2, "*God has not rejected his people whom <u>he foreknew</u> (Israel). Do you not know what the Scripture says of Elijah, how he appeals to God against Israel?*" ESV. So God foreknew and predestined, not Gentiles or Christians, but the children of Israel who he called, justified and glorified. In fact, the "adoption of sons," is also found

---

[75] Romans 3:2

in [76]Romans. Paul again speaking about Israel says, "*who are Israelites, to whom belongs the adoption as sons, and the glory and the covenants and the giving of the Law and the temple service and the promises,* " NASB. Paul concludes this in Romans 11:5 and is not referring to an elect chosen group for eternal life but a remnant of Jewish believers by God's choice, "*In the same way then, there has also come to be at the present time a remnant according to God's gracious choice.*" NASB. Paul then switches from Jews to Gentiles in Romans 11:11-13 as the readers who now need to listen. This is never discussed among Calvinist because it would destroy their whole concept of Reform theology and how God elects believers for salvation.

    This takes us right back to Ephesians 1:3-11. We now know who Paul is speaking about in regards to terms like "chose us," "predestined," "foreknew" and "adoption as son." Even verse 9 is part of the Amidah prayer which says, "*You favor humanity with knowledge and teach people understanding. Favor us with knowledge, understanding and insight from yourself. Praised be you,*

---

[76] Romans 9:4

Adonai, gracious Giver of knowledge." There can be little doubt about Ephesians 1:3-11 being spoken directly to the Jewish people and Israel and not to Christian believers who have been elected by God for eternal life through Jesus. If there is still doubt then verse 13 should clear it all up. *"In Him, you also, after listening to the message of truth, the gospel of your salvation – having also believed, you were sealed in Him with the Holy Spirit of promise,"* NASB. Who is the *"you also"* that Paul is referring? They are the [77]Gentiles in the flesh who are uncircumcised and who did not know God or his covenants and who were far off from God, strangers. They were now brought near by the blood of Yeshua-Jesus. The Jew and the Gentile are now [78]one new man in Yeshua- Jesus.

    Why do Dr. White and others ignore all this from Scripture? I cannot fully say, but I can tell you that how Dr. White and other Reform teachers interpret Ephesian 1:3-11 and all the other texts we already mentioned are in error. They all fail to look at the

---

[77] Ephesians 2:11-13

[78] Ephesians 2:15

Hebrew Scriptures for comparison, Jewish sources for understanding and the historical context and setting for interpretation. As I said before, a person cannot look at the Bible and assume everything written in it is directed to the reader because they see "you," "we," or "us" in the passage. That is a poor way to exegete the Bible.

Romans 9: Salvation or Judgment?

As we have already established, Romans chapters 7:1-11:13, are speaking directly to the Jews and not to the Gentiles. Therefore we must examine chapter 9 as referencing the Jews and Israel. To do differently would be a violation of the Scriptures. Within the chapters of 7 through 11 we read keywords that are only related the Jews and Israel. We read "Torah/Law," "foreknew," "adoption," "chosen," and "predestination." All of which are described as for the Jews. One just needs to read Romans 8:26 with Romans 9:11:2 to see this example. Romans 8:26 describes God who foreknew and predestined Israel and the Jews. How do I know? Well according to Romans 11:2 Paul says, *"God has not rejected his people whom he foreknew. Do you not know what the Scripture says of Elijah, how he appeals to God against Israel?"* So God foreknew, predestined and chose his people Israel to bring redemption to his creation through his son, Yeshua-Jesus. There should be no doubt of this basic pashat (simple reading) of the text.

Calvinist and Reformers turn Romans chapter 9 into a very complex chapter when a direct and simple reading with a comparison to the Hebrew Old Testament is all that is needed. Paul begins Romans chapter 9 with great sorrow for his kin and brothers in the flesh who are Israelites. Paul wishes to be under the physical curse of God and possibly die so that Israel will be delivered from what is about to come upon them as a nation. This [79]curse is referenced in the Torah against Israel. Paul is building the case that just because the Jews are part of Israel and the 12 tribes in the flesh with the Messiah does not mean they are truly from Israel. We see this example in John 8:33;38 where the Jewish leaders tell Yeshua-Jesus, *"We are Abraham's*

---

[79] Leviticus 26:14-39; Deuteronomy 28:15-68.

descendants...Abraham is our father." Yeshua-Jesus rebukes their claim and tells them they are the father of the accuser or devil. So Paul is correct in Romans 9:6-7 where he finishes with, *"and not all are children of Abraham because they are his seed, but "Through Isaac shall your seed be named."* So it is the children of the promise and not the flesh who are regarded as part of the seed of Abraham. Paul starts with Sarah and the promise of Isaac and then Rebekah who would have Jacob and Esau. Rebekah asked the Lord about the struggle within her womb in Genesis 25:22. The Lord [80]replied, *"And the LORD said to her, "Two nations are in your womb, and two peoples from within you shall be divided; the one shall be stronger than the other, the older shall serve the younger."* God had made his choice, and Paul confirms this in Romans 9:11. But did God really "hate" Esau?

Paul goes on to quote Malachi 1:2-3 where God is speaking to Israel through Malachi. Israel while being in exile ask the Lord how he has loved them? They are judged and are in exile from God. Yet God answers with, *"Was not Esau Jacob's brother? saith the*

---

[80] Genesis 25:23

LORD; yet I loved Jacob, But Esau I hated, and made his mountains a desolation, and gave his heritage to the jackals of the wilderness."* JPS. The Hebrew and Aramaic for "hated" is better translated as "turned away from" or "rejected" from and by God. God is speaking, not to the person but to the nation Israel as a promise through Jacob who is also Israel. God rejected Esau for the promise of the seed or Messiah, and by his choice, he gave the promise to Jacob. Nothing is speaking of an individual promise of salvation or eternal life by God's choice. To make this even more clear about God speaking about the people of Israel Paul quotes Exodus 33:19 where we read how Moses is pleading with God to show mercy and grace to his people. Moses asked God on his behalf, *"...and consider that this nation is Thy people."* JPS. Moses continues to plead with God for his people until God answers, [81]*" 'I will make all My goodness pass before thee, and will proclaim the name of the LORD before thee, and I will be gracious to whom I will be gracious, and will show mercy on whom I will show mercy.'"* JPS. This has nothing to do with God choosing who will be

---

[81] Exodus 33:19

saved or receive eternal life. This is about how he has established Israel as a people and how he will continue to judge them for their rejection of Moses and Yeshua-Jesus.

Paul then brings a stronger argument for God's mercy by using Pharaoh as an example. Instead of striking down Pharaoh and Egypt right away God shows his mercy by allowing Pharaoh to remain in power. *"For by now I could have put out my hand and struck you and your people with pestilence, and you would have been cut off from the earth. But for this purpose I have raised you up, to show you my power, so that my name may be proclaimed in all the earth."* The story of Pharaoh has been discussed earlier but to recap we must understand that God told Moses that Pharaoh would not let his people go unless under a strong hand. But God will also hold Pharaoh back from releasing them too early so that his power will be known to the world and mercy will be shown by not destroying them right away. Once again, Romans 9 is not speaking about how God saves an individual but how God deals with Israel and the nations regarding how he judges them based on his will and not ours. There is nothing in Romans 9 that even mentions eternal life or salvation. This is assumed by Calvinist and Reformers based on a faulty interpretation and a failure to exam the Hebrew OT references used by Paul in their proper context.

The final proof for Paul speaking about the coming judgment on Israel is found in Romans 9:20-24. Paul refers to Jeremiah 18:4-10 to show how God deals with a nation like Israel and the men of Judah. The key passage in Jeremiah 18 is verse 4, *"But the vessel that he was making of clay was <u>spoiled</u> in the hand of the potter; so he remade it into another vessel, as it pleased the potter to make."* What Calvinist and Reformers ignore is the word [82]"spoiled" in Hebrew. This illustration by Jeremiah explains how the clay (Israel) is acting corruptly in the hand of the potter, so he destroys it and remakes it to please him. This is explained further in Jeremiah [83]18 when we read, *"At one moment I might speak concerning a nation or concerning a kingdom to uproot, to pull down, or to destroy it; if that nation against*

---

[82] NASEC: Shachath-to go to ruin: — act corruptly, שחת

[83] Jeremiah 18:7-10

which I have spoken turns from its evil, I will relent concerning the calamity I planned to bring on it. "Or at another moment I might speak concerning a nation or concerning a kingdom to build up or to plant it; if it does evil in My sight by not obeying My voice, then I will think better of the good with which I had promised to bless it. "So now then, speak to the men of Judah and against the inhabitants of Jerusalem saying, 'Thus says the LORD, "Behold, I am fashioning calamity against you and devising a plan against you. Oh turn back, each of you from his evil way, and reform your ways and your deeds."' The whole context of Jeremiah is not about individual salvation or eternal life but how God deals with Israel and Judah regarding judgment as a nation. This is why Paul refers back to Jeremiah 18 and discusses two vessels in Romans 9. The vessel (Israel) acted corruptly against God, but God showed mercy by not destroying Israel immediately, but with patience, he waited and sent his son Yeshua-Jesus to call them to repentance. Israel and Judah were already prepared for destruction for their rejection of Moses and then Yeshua-Jesus. This is why Yeshua-

Jesus [84]wept over Jerusalem because he knew what was going to come upon them within 40 years. This was already prophesied by [85]Daniel. The second vessel was called by God from among Jews and Gentiles to be vessels of glory and mercy from God. Paul quotes Hosea 2:23 and Hosea 1:10 immediately after discussing the vessels for mercy and glory. But the final nail is when Paul quotes Isaiah 10:22 to show how a remnant among Israel that will be delivered from the coming judgment.

If we are fair to the context of Romans 9 and refer to the Hebrew Old Testament for complete context as to what Paul is trying to say to the Jews, then there is no way someone can think that Paul is talking about salvation among some elect. Again, the context, historical setting, and the Hebrew Scriptures with pashat (simple reading) cannot be ignored by Calvinist or Reformers.

---

[84] Luke 19:41-44

[85] Daniel 9:24-27

CONCLUSION

The Calvinists and Reformers need to really consider their position in regards on how God truly deals with his people in the Hebrew Old Testament and how God truly saves those who believe in his son Yeshua-Jesus. Individuals are not selected by God for eternal life, and all the others are passed up by God and are judged to eternal separation from God. We all have a choice that was received by the fall. We have been given the ability to discern good from evil, to choose life or death. We can seek God and do good or reject God and do evil. If we have faith in God through his son Yeshua-Jesus, then we can continue to do good for the blessings, or we can turn from God and receive his curses which leads to death. This should not be a debate of Calvinism vs. Arminianism. My position is one that brings both views together. God is in total control of his creation, but when it comes to an individuals choice to follow his commandments or to reject them, we are responsible for that choice. This is how the Bible explains man's sin after the fall about his inclination toward doing good or evil. From Noah to Moses and the Prophets, we can see how God can tell his people to return to him for life and blessings or face the curses of death and exile. The Jews have always believed in God's sovereignty while holding on to an individual's right to choose to do good or evil. We saw this in the Hebrew Bible, Jewish sources, and in the New Testament when connected with the Hebrew Old Testament. We cannot believe a doctrine formed hundreds or even over a thousand years later and then try to interpret the Bible based on those late teachings. Calvinism must be challenged based on its failure to look at the Hebrew Scriptures, Jewish sources, the historical context and setting of the Old and the New Testament. Please remember, this is not an issue of whether someone is saved or not saved because they believe or do not believe in Calvinism. We should consider this matter a non-essential discussion and not be afraid to engage in a respectful debate or discussion on these issues. I hope this book helped someone in understanding why both Calvinism and Arminianism are right when examined together. God bless.

APPENDIX A

John 1:11-13

In this appendix will look at John 1:11-13 which Calvinist use to support that it is by God's will that man is born again and not by man's own will. Here is the verse in question.

"He came to his own, and his own people did not receive him. But to all who did receive him, who believed in his name, he gave the right to become children of God, who were born, not of blood nor of the will of the flesh nor of the will of man, but of God." (ESV Translation)

Greek

εις τα ιδια ηλθεν και οι ιδιοι αυτον ου παρελαβον οσοι δε ελαβον αυτον εδωκεν αυτοις εξουσιαν τεκνα θεου γενεσθαι τοις πιστευουσιν εις το ονομα αυτου οι ουκ εξ αιματων ουδε εκ θεληματος σαρκος ουδε εκ θεληματος ανδρος αλλ εκ θεου εγεννηθησαν. (Greek TR)

The first part of these verses that we must look at is verse 11 and the context of 11-13. Jesus came to his own, *hoi idioi,* which refers to "his own family" or "his own friends." We see this again in John 13:1, *"...having loved His own..."* This is reflective of the Jewish people, the chosen people. In Matthew 15:24 we read, *"But He answered and said, "I was sent only to the lost sheep of the house of Israel."* His own people did not receive him or welcome him as the Greek implies. The Greek phrase, *auton ou parelabon,* is the second aorist active indicative of *paralambanō.* This is a common Greek verb for "welcome" or to take a side. Yeshua-Jesus' own people did not welcome or receive him as the Jewish Messiah.

The next verse, verse 12, connects 11 with, *"But as many as received Him,"* and has similar Greek usage with *hosoi elabon auton* which is an aorist active indicative of *lambanō*-*"as many as did receive him,"* in contrast with *hoi idioi* just before. Those who took hold of him and accepted Yeshua-Jesus as Messiah, to them God gave the right to become children of God, to those who believed in his name. The authority was given to the Jews first and foremost, Romans 2:10. There is no mention of non-Jews or Gentiles in the first two verses, 11-12, by John. Although the term *"to those who believe"* is a present participle, which reflects those who conitinue to believe in his name, there is no certain view in mind in regards if Gentiles were included in this passage. We can assume the possibility that they were but the context is clear. It was some of his own people who rejected him but those who did receive him and believe on his name, they were given the authority to be sons of God. So what about verse 13?

In verse 13 we continue to read the action of God toward the those who believed, namely his people. *"who were born, not of blood nor of the will of the flesh nor of the will of man, but of God."* (ESV Translation). This verse should give us a reflection of John 3:3 where Yeshua-Jesus tells Nicodemus, *"Truly, truly, I say to you, unless one is born again he cannot see the kingdom of God... Truly, truly, I say to you, unless one is born of water and the Spirit, he cannot enter the kingdom of God... That which is born of the flesh is flesh, and that which is born of the Spirit is spirit...that whoever believes in him may have eternal life."* (ESV Translation). The best reading in connecting 12 and 13 should be, *"he gave the right to become children of God, who were born of God. Not of blood nor of the will of the flesh nor of the will of man."* This does not have to mean election or predestined to become children of God but can mean that are actions do not save us, only the actions of God who sent his son to die for our sins and those who believe on him and his name will be saved. To assume the *elect* is reading into the text what is not there or made clear. God is the source of our salvation, but the cause behind his action is clear in the other passages of verse 11-12. So there is nothing we can do physically to be saved. Nor does it matter how you were born in regards to lineage. The Pharisees argued their lineage being from Abraham. None of this matter but only the completed work of Yeshua-Jesus which give us the opportunity to believe and receive his finished work on the cross.

APPENDIX B

Acts 13:48

This next verse is used by Calvinist to firmly demonstrate that God "ordains" and "appoints" people to eternal life which then cause them to believe and trust in him. But is that really what the verse is saying? What about the context of the chapter? Let us first look at the verse in question.

"When the Gentiles heard this, they began rejoicing and glorifying the word of the Lord; and as many as had been appointed to eternal life believed." (NASB Translation)

ἀκούοντα δὲ τὰ ἔθνη ἔχαιρον καὶ ἐδόξαζον τὸν λόγον τοῦ Κυρίου, καὶ ἐπίστευσαν ὅσοι ἦσαν τεταγμένοι εἰς ζωὴν αἰώνιον· (Greek Translation)

All Greek scholars agree that Luke is using the imperfect form of *eimi* with a perfect passive participle. This means that the phrase, *"as many as had been appointed to eternal life"* is a pluperfect in Greek. This demonstrates a completed action in the past and does not mean a continuation of the past action into the present time. Calvinist will argue that this is proof of God's eternal decree to appoint individuals to eternal life. But is this true? Is this what Luke meant?

First, let me quotes [86]Dr. Daniel B. Wallace on the definition of *pluperfect* and how it is understood in the Greek. *"The pluperfect combines the aspects of the aorist (for the event) and the imperfect (for the results). To put this another way, the force of the pluperfect tense is that it describes an event that, completed in the past, has results that existed in the past as well (in relation to the time of speaking). The pluperfect makes no comment about the results existing up to the time of speaking. Such results may exist at the time of speaking or they may not; the pluperfect contributes nothing either way. (Often, however, it can be ascertained from the context whether or not the results do indeed exist up to the time of speaking.)* So, do we have an event to look at that gives us the results described in Acts 13:48? Let us consider the context for the answer.

Paul was at the synagogue in Pisidian Antioch on the Sabbath. He stood up and gave an argument

---

[86] *Greek Grammar Beyond the Basics*, pg.583. Daniel B. Wallace

regarding the prophecies of the Hebrew Scriptures concerning Yeshua-Jesus being the Messiah. He concludes with saying, *"and in Him (Yeshua-Jesus) everyone who believes is justified from all things."* The people begged Paul and Barnabas to return the next Sabbath and speak to them. Many Jews and proselytes followed Paul and Barnabas after they finished at the synagogue. On the next Sabbath, almost the whole city gathered to hear Paul speak on the Word of the Lord. The "whole city" reflects the fact that Gentiles also came to hear Paul. Other Jews who saw the crowds got jealous and began to slander Paul and contradict him. Paul speaks out against the Jews who were slandering him by saying, *"It was necessary that the word of God be spoken to you first; since you repudiate it and judge yourselves unworthy of eternal life, behold, we are turning to the Gentiles. For so the Lord has commanded us, 'I HAVE PLACED YOU AS A LIGHT FOR THE GENTILES, THAT YOU MAY BRING SALVATION TO THE END OF THE EARTH'"* (NASB Translation). This now brings us to verse 48 of Acts 13. *"When the Gentiles heard this, they began rejoicing and glorifying the word of the Lord; and as many as had been appointed to eternal life believed."*

We have the answer to what Dr. Wallace describes in his definition of *pluperfect*. "*the force of the pluperfect tense is that it describes an event that, completed in the past, has results that existed in the past as well (in relation to the time of speaking).*" The results in the past are not part of the pluperfect, and it does not comment on the results existing. But the context can give us the results in the past if they exist leading up to the time of speaking. The answer is found in the Hebrew Scriptures quoted by Paul in verse 47, "*I will make you as a light for the nations, that my salvation may reach to the end of the earth.*" (Isaiah 49:6 ESV) This was also fulfilled when Simeon, in Luke 2:25-32, declared after seeing the Messiah as promised that, "*For my eyes have seen Your salvation(Yeshua), Which You have prepared in the presence of all peoples, 'A LIGHT OF REVELATION TO THE GENTILES, And the glory of Your people Israel.'*" We have what is missing and what the pluperfect does not tell us, that the action completed in the past is found in Isaiah 49:6 and Luke 2:25-32. Acts 13:48 was not an eternal decree by God about appointing individuals to eternal life. Acts 13:48 was a continued fulfillment of Isaiah 49:6, in verse 47, spoken by Paul and also fulfilled in Luke 2 with Simeon's announcement. Let us now look at Acts 13:48 correctly and in light of what we now know from Isaiah 49:6.

1. Paul quotes Isaiah 49:6 which says that "eternal life" will include the Gentiles and fulfilled in Luke 2:30-32.

2. With that fulfilled prophecy, God through Isaiah had "appointed" Gentiles, not all, to eternal life.

3. The Gentiles heard this and began glorifying and praising the "Word of God." Those who were (2a.) "appointed" to eternal life, through the fulfilled prophecy of Isaiah and Luke, they believed.

That is how Acts 13:48 should be understood and read based on Greek grammar. It is NOT speaking about individuals being predestined to eternal life. This is speaking about a collective group within the Nations or Gentiles who were spoken about in Isaiah. Those Gentiles fulfilled Isaiah and Luke's "appointed to eternal life" by hearing, praising and believing. This answers the pluperfect participle in Acts 13:48 in the Greek. Calvinist fail at looking at the context and connecting passages found in the Hebrew Bible and in the New Testament. Acts 13:48 is the springboard for showing how the Gentiles are now worthy of eternal life without becoming a proselyte first. A proselyte is a Gentile who converts to Judaism and all its practices. This conversion was not necessary now and discussed later in Acts 15.

We now see the true understanding of Acts 13:48 in its complete context and historical reference to Isaiah and also found in Luke 2. There should be no confusion how the Gentiles were "appointed" to eternal life by believing what they just heard from Paul. Calvinist will continue to use "one-liners" in the Bible to try and prove their position but fail to look at the context, historical background, setting, and language correctly.

If we consider the other verses used by Calvinist like Matthew 11:25-37; John 5:21; Romans 1:1 etc. you will recognize the error of not looking at the context of the verses used nor its background regarding who is spoken to in the context. This is a theme in Calvinism.

BIBLIOGRAPHY

Hebrew Language

William Chomsky, *Hebrew: The Eternal Language.* Philadelphia: Jewish Publication Society, 1957.

Edward Y. Kutscher, *A History of the Hebrew language*, edited by Raphael Kutscher. Jerusalem: Magnes Press, Hebrew University, 1982. 306 pages. ISBN: 9652233978.

Henry Craik, *The Hebrew Language: Its History and Characteristics, Including Improved Renderings of Select Passages in our Authorized Translation of the Old Testament.* London: Bagster, 1860. 187 pages.

Texts

Jacob ben Hayyin, ed., *Biblia Rabbinica*: A Reprint of the 1525 Venice Edition. Four volumes. Jerusalem: Makor Publishing, 1972. A reprint of the Rabbinic Bible originally published by Daniel Bomberg in Venice.

Aharon Dotan, ed. *Biblia Hebraica Leningradensia*, Prepared according to the Vocalization, Accents, and Masora of Aaron ben Moses ben Asher in the Leningrad Codex. Peabody, Mass: Hendrickson Publishers, 2001.

Norman H. Snaith, *Sefer Torah, Nevi'im u-Khetuvim* [title transliterated from Hebrew script]. London: British and Foreign Bible Society, 1958. Reprinted under the title The Hebrew Scriptures. ISBN: 0564000299.

Meïr Letters, ed., *The Holy Scriptures of the Old Testament, Hebrew and English.* London: British and Foreign Bible Society, 1866. Often reprinted.

The JPS Hebrew-English Tanakh. Philadelphia: Jewish Publication Society, 1999. ISBN: 0827606567.

Hebrew-English Interlinear Editions
John R. Kohlenberger III, ed., *The NIV Interlinear Hebrew-English Old Testament.* Grand Rapids: Zondervan, 1979-85.

Concordances
John R. Kohlenberger III and James A. Swanson, *The Hebrew English Concordance to the Old Testament with the New International Version.* Grand Rapids: Zondervan, 1998. 2192 pages.

Abraham Even-Shoshan, *A New Concordance of the Old Testament.* Grand Rapids: Baker, 1989.

Lexicons
Francis Brown, Samuel R. Driver, and Charles A. Briggs, eds., *A Hebrew and English Lexicon of the Old Testament.* Oxford: Clarendon Press, 1906. Corrected edition, 1952. Known by the abbreviation BDB. Still the standard lexicon in English.

William L. Holladay, ed., *A Concise Hebrew and Aramaic Lexicon of the Old Testament,* based on the Lexical Work of Ludwig Koehler and Walter Baumgartner. Grand Rapids: Eerdmans, 1971. 425 pages.

Wilhelm Gesenius, *Gesenius' Hebrew and Chaldee Lexicon to the Old Testament Scriptures.* Translated with additions from the author's Thesaurus and works, by S. P. Tregelles. London: Samuel Bagster & Sons, 1846.

David J. A. Clines, ed., *The Dictionary of Classical Hebrew.* Eight Vols. Scheduled (Sheffield Academic Press, 1993-present). The first volume 1993, vol.2 in 1995, vol. 3 in 1996, vol. 4 in 1998, vol. 5 in 2001, vol. 6 in 2003.

Hebrew and Jewish Culture
William Smith, Smith's *Bible Dictionary* (Grand Rapids, Mi.: Zondervan, 1948)

J.I. Packer, Merril C. Tenney, William White, Jr., *Nelson's Illustrated Encyclopedia of Bible Facts* (Nashville: Thomas Nelson, 1995)

Madelene S. Miller and J. Lane Miller, *Harper's Bible Dictionary*, (New York, Harper, 1973)

Henry H. Halley, *Halley's Bible Handbook*(Grand Rapids, Mi: Zondervan, 24th)

The New Westminster Dictionary of the Bible (Philidelphia, Westminster, 1976)

NIV Compact Dictionary of the Bible, (Grand Rapids, Zondervan, 1989)

The Lion Encyclopedia of the Bible, (Tring, Lion, 1986)

Fred H. Wight, *Manners, and Customs of Bible Lands* (Chicago: Moody, 1983)

Madeleine S. Miller and J. Lane Miller, *Encyclopedia of Bible Life* (New York: Harper & Brothers, 1944)

Segal, Alan F. Two Powers In Heaven: The Baylor University Press, Waco Texas 2012 reprint.

Hebrew Word Studies
James Strong, *New Strong's Concise Dictionary of the Words in the Hebrew Bible*, (Nashville, Nelson, 1995)

W. E. Vine, Merrill F. Unger, William White, *Vine's Expository Dictionary of Biblical Words*, (Nashville, Nelson,

1985)

Benjamin Davidson, *The Analytical Hebrew and Chaldee Lexicon*, (London, Samuel Bagster)

Isaac Mozeson *The Word: the Dictionary that reveals the Hebrew origin of English* (New York. S.P.I. Books, Inc.)

Ehud Ben-Yehuda, David Weinstein, *English-Hebrew Hebrew-English Dictionary*, (N.Y., Washington Square Press, Inc., 1961)

Rev. Walter W. Skeat, *A Concise Etymological Dictionary of the English* Language, (N.Y., Capricorn Books, 1963)

Tsvi Sadan, *The Concealed Light; Names of Messiah in Jewish Sources*, (Vine of David, First Fruits of Zion, Inc. 2012)

Ancient Languages and their Origin
John Philip Cohane *The Key*, (N.Y., Crown Publishers, 1969)

Charlton Laird *The Miracle of Language* (Greenwich Conn., Fawcett, 1953)

Giorgio Fano, *The Origins and Nature of Language*, (Bloomington In., Indiana University Press, 1992)

Isaac.E Mozeson, *The Origin of Speeches* 2nd edition, Lightcatcher Books, Springdale, AR ISBN 0-9792618-0-5

Calvinism
Loraine Boettner. *"The Perseverance of the Saints."* The Reformed Doctrine of Predestination.

James R.White. *"The Potter's Freedom"* Calvery Press.

John Piper. *"The Justification of God"* Second Edition. Baker Academic.

Livingstone, Elizabeth A. (2005). "Original sin." *The Oxford dictionary of the Christian Church* (3rd ed.). Oxford: Oxford University Press.

Sproul, R C *(1997). What is Reformed Theology?*. Grand Rapids: Baker Books.

www.ingramcontent.com/pod-product-compliance
Lightning Source LLC
LaVergne TN
LVHW051843080426
835512LV00018B/3048